e.g.sheppardmoscow

Sheppard Moscow Ireland Ltd
2nd Floor, Suite 32, The Mall
Beacon Court, Sandyford, Dublin 18

Changing Conversations in Organizations

Drawing on the theoretical foundations laid out in earlier volumes of the series, this book describes an approach to organizational change and development informed by a complexity perspective. It sets out to make sense of the experience of being *in the midst of change*. Unlike many books that presume clarity of foresight or hindsight, the author focuses on the essential uncertainty of participating in evolving events as they happen and enquires into the creative possibilities of such participation.

The book questions the way much thinking about organizational change suggests that we can choose and design new futures for our organizations in the way we often hope. Avoiding the widely favoured use of 2 by 2 matrices, idealized schemas and simplified typologies that characterize much of the management literature on change, this book encourages the reader to live with the immediate paradoxes and complexities of organizational life, where we must act with intention into the unknowable. The author uses detailed reflective narrative to evoke and elaborate on the experience of participating attentively in the conversational processes of human organizing. It takes as central the conversational life of organizations as the activity in which we perpetually sustain and change the possibilities for going on together.

This book will be valuable to consultants, managers and leaders, indeed all those who are dissatisfied with idealized models of change and are searching for ways to develop as effective practitioners seeking to contribute to the evolution of the organizations they work with.

Patricia Shaw is a visiting professor at the University of Hertfordshire where she co-founded the Complexity and Management Centre. As an organizational consultant for nearly twenty years, she has moved away from large-scale change programmes towards more conversational approaches to learning whereby spontaneity, improvisation and lively sense-making may flourish amidst everyday politics and conflict.

Complexity and Emergence in Organizations

Series editors:
Ralph D. Stacey, Douglas Griffin and **Patricia Shaw**

The books in this series each give expression to a particular way of speaking about complexity in organizations. Drawing on insights from the complexity sciences, psychology and sociology, this series aims to provide a whole spectrum of theories of human organization, including ethics.

Titles in this series include:

Complexity and Management
Fad or radical challenge to systems thinking?
Ralph D. Stacey, Douglas Griffin and Patricia Shaw

Complex Responsive Processes
Learning and knowledge creation
Ralph D. Stacey

The Paradox of Control in Organizations
Philip J. Streatfield

Complexity and Innovation in Organizations
José Fonseca

The Emergence of Leadership
Linking self-organization and ethics
Douglas Griffin

Changing Conversations in Organizations
A complexity approach to change
Patricia Shaw

Changing Conversations in Organizations

A complexity approach to change

Patricia Shaw

London and New York

First published 2002
by Routledge
11 New Fetter Lane, London EC4P 4EE

Simultaneously published in the USA and Canada
by Routledge
29 West 35th Street, New York, NY 10001

Routledge is an imprint of the Taylor & Francis Group

Typeset in Times New Roman by Wearset Ltd, Boldon, Tyne and Wear
Printed and bound in Great Britain by MPG Books Ltd, Bodmin

British Library Cataloguing in Publication Data
A catalogue record for this book is available from the British Library

Library of Congress Cataloging in Publication Data
A catalog record has been requested

ISBN 0-415-24915-5 (hbk)
ISBN 0-415-24914-7 (pbk)

To
Luke and Michael
with whom it's always good to talk

Contents

Series preface
Complexity and Emergence in Organizations

The aim of this series is to give expression to a particular way of speaking about complexity in organizations, one that emphasizes the self-referential, reflexive nature of humans, the essentially responsive and participative nature of human processes of relating and the radical unpredictability of their evolution. It draws on the complexity sciences, which can be brought together with psychology and sociology in many different ways to form a whole spectrum of theories of human organization.

At one end of this spectrum there is the dominant voice in organization and management theory, which speaks in the language of design, regularity and control. In this language, managers stand outside the organizational system, which is thought of as an objective, pre-given reality that can be modelled and designed, and they control it. Managers here are concerned with the functional aspects of a system as they search for causal links that promise sophisticated tools for predicting its behaviour. The dominant voice talks about the individual as autonomous, self-contained, masterful and at the centre of an organization. Many complexity theorists talk in a language that is immediately compatible with this dominant voice. They talk about complex adaptive systems as networks of autonomous agents that behave on the basis of regularities extracted, from their environments. They talk about complex systems as objective realities that scientists can stand back from and model. They emphasize the predictable aspects of these systems and see their modelling work as a route to increasing the ability of humans to control complex worlds.

At the other end of the spectrum there are voices from the fringes of organizational theory, complexity sciences, psychology and sociology which are defining a participative perspective. They argue that humans are themselves members of the complex networks that they form and are drawing attention to the impossibility of standing outside of them in order to objectify and model them. With this intersubjective voice people speak as subjects interacting with others in the co-evolution of a jointly constructed reality. These voices emphasize the radically unpredictable aspects of self-organizing processes and their creative potential. These are the voices of decentred agency, which talk about agents and the social world in which they live as mutually created and sustained. This way of thinking weaves together relationship psychologies and the work of complexity theorists who focus on the emergent and radically unpredictable aspects of complex systems. The result is a participative approach to understanding the complexities of organizational life.

This series is intended to give expression to the second of these voices, defining a participative perspective.

Series editors
Ralph D. Stacey, Douglas Griffin, Patricia Shaw
Complexity and Management Centre,
University of Hertfordshire

1 Changing conversations

- What has 'facilitation' come to mean?
- The legacy of process consultation and organization development
- Conversing as organizing, organizing as conversing
- The value of 'just talking'
- Glimpsing another way of working
- A complexity approach to change

I began to ask myself what kind of work I was doing as an organizational consultant, when I found that from time to time I was being accused, albeit with curiosity, of not being a 'proper' consultant, or coach, or facilitator. Whether in relation to longer assignments or single encounters, the comments often seemed to be in response to what I was *not* doing. I did not write formal proposals for work. I did not prepare detailed designs for meetings, conferences, workshops. I did not develop detailed aims and objectives in advance. I did not clarify roles and expectations or agree ground rules at the start of working. I did not hold back my views or opinions. I did not develop clear action plans at the end of meetings. I did not capture outcomes. I failed to encourage 'feedback' or behavioural contracting between people. I did not 'manage' process. There seemed to be a lot of things that I did not do that most people had come to expect. At the same time, many managers seemed frustrated with the other forms of consulting or with the facilitation of some other meetings they had taken part in. They said *approvingly* that I was unlike most consultants they had worked with, although they were hard put to express more precisely what they valued about my contribution.

What has 'facilitation' come to mean?

In French or Italian, the word *facile* means 'simple, easy, no fuss needed', but in English it is not really a compliment, carrying a sense of something rendered too easy, almost glib. If someone accuses another of making a facile remark they might be suggesting that significant complexities are being underplayed. Maybe they also feel stung, possibly hurt, certainly irritated. So the implication is that the word 'facile' is used when someone is not altogether off track but has reduced or caricatured issues in some way that the accuser finds insensitive, even crass. For me, this sense of the word lurks around some kinds of facilitation intended in a positive sense to help complicated, difficult, conflictual situations of human engagement flow more easily and productively. So how have I developed this uneasy sense of some facilitation and process consultation as facile? Although I still call myself an organization development consultant, I am aware of how much the way I work has diverged from what this term has come to mean. This is not just in relation to fellow consulting professionals, but to large numbers of managers and executives who are asked to become enabling or facilitative leaders.

So my first aim in this chapter is to look at how approaches that emerged as a fresh impetus in organizations in the 1960s and 1970s may have congealed into habitual patterns of response. Yet I also want to keep in mind how the conversations that recreate these habitual patterns also have the potential for evolving novel forms of practice.

Recently I agreed at short notice to help a central marketing group in a large organization that I have been working with for some time. The members of the group were about to meet to discuss a new framework for their *raison d'être* that was being developed by two consultants from a well-known management consulting firm. I was asked to a meeting with the consultants and two senior members of the new team a few days before the strategic meeting of the whole group. The consultants had prepared a set of power-point slides that the manager of the team would be using to provide an introduction and overview of the proposed session. I was taken through the slides, one at a time:

> Exercise 1: *Expectations*. Log on flip chart everyone's expectations of the meeting. No right or wrong answers.
> Exercise 2: *Unspoken agendas*. Bring out people's issues, fears, obstacles to working as a team. Good to express unspoken feelings but needs to stay within certain productive boundaries.

> Team leader to communicate Long-Term Vision and high level objectives. Feedback from group about their roles, where can they add value, their deliverables. Team buy-in.

> Exercise 3: *Partner needs*. List and rank in order of importance the primary needs of internal and external partners and customers.

Exercise 4: *Brainstorming*. Conduct brainstorming to identify initiatives that should be considered in first 18 months.

Exercise 5: *Value*. For each initiative identify primary points of value for our partners and customers.

Exercise 6: *Prioritization*. Prioritize initiatives by placing in quadrants of 2 by 2 matrix labelled Business Impact – High/low against Ease of Implementation – High/low. Select short list of initiatives with timings for implementation for next four quarters.

Exercise 7: *Performance measures*. Identify appropriate performance measures for planned initiatives.

Exercise 8: *Value proposition*. For each internal and external partner or customer, list points of value under Functional benefits (rational) and Emotional benefits.

Exercise 9: *Fit*. Explore how to work within SM and Group marketing to create synergy and leverage resources.

Exercise 10: *Rules of engagement*. Determine the rules that will create a positive and engaging work environment.

Review: Deliverables, actions and plans moving forward. Log unresolved issues and possible solutions with clear direction for follow-up.

It was clearly expected that I 'facilitate' the group as they worked through this agenda, with some fluidity, of course, around the exact order and timing of the exercises. Perhaps we would not need them all. As I listened, a feeling of dissonance was growing. What seemed strange to me was very familiar to the others. 'Look,' I said, 'I just don't work this way at all. I don't really understand what you want me for. You've got a very clear structure for the meeting and two consultants to help the group work through this agenda, if that's what everyone wants to do.' 'No, no,' said the consultants, 'our role is to help the group work with the business model, not to facilitate the meeting.' The woman who had first asked me to join the meeting said, 'Some of the discussion could be charged, that's what we want you to handle.'

Silently I was already arguing about the whole rationale implicit so far. I did not voice this but turned to the team leader and asked in a conversational tone whether he could keep these slides as back up and start the meeting by talking with the group about how things stood so far, what was on his mind at this point, what he felt needed discussion at this meeting, and so on. The manager, replied that, certainly, he could do that. 'Then couldn't we just see how others responded and take things from there?' I suggested.

There was a pause in which I felt I had said something naïve and, embarrassing and, indeed, in a way I had. By using the word 'just' I was in danger of implying that there was nothing to be understood in a suggestion that we 'take things from there'. My aim in this book will be to draw attention to the complex social processes involved in 'going on together from here' and to talk about the ordinary artistry of our joint participation in these processes. In the pause I fancy we were all imagining the unknowable particulars of this future engagement, the proposed meeting, and what might flow from it. The question was, how would we approach this uncertainty?

The other team member came in: 'This is the kind of structure we always use to ensure a productive meeting.' 'But look at this item,' I said: 'Unspoken agendas. Don't you think there is something quite funny about having that as an agenda item?' She looked a little offended for a moment, yet also seeing what I meant. 'Yes, but that's your job, to help get out the hidden agendas early so that they don't get in the way of the meeting later on.' I recognized this conundrum. We have all experienced the way that, as a meeting progresses we or others may express what we now assume we might usefully have expressed earlier, but didn't. Surely we can get a grip on this problem. Now that we realize what it would have been useful to know earlier, can't we ensure that next time we get everything out in the right order!

At that point I relaxed in my seat and again sought an everyday way of expressing myself:

> What I'm trying to say is that I can see that this is a crucial meeting. There hasn't been a central marketing group before, there must be a lot of pressure to succeed, people must be uncertain how best to take up their new responsibilities and how best to contribute to the business. You've put aside a couple of days for an in-depth discussion of the issues facing you and how you go forward. There's been a lot of preparatory conversations and documentation that will feed into the meeting. I would be very happy to join you and help to find whatever form of conversation we need as things develop.

There was a palpable rise in temperature all round. 'That's exactly what we want,' said the manager, looking pleased and relieved.

To me this example shows very clearly what has happened in the corporate world. Decades of a certain kind of business school education and writing; the rise and rise of expensive management consulting focused on packaging 'best practice' and promising to provide the

expertise that will 'deliver' desired future success; the professionalization
of all kinds of human communication into codified behavioural notions
of 'coaching', 'counselling', 'teamwork' or 'leading' – all these have
given us a curiously rational, instrumental approach to ourselves. In the
short encounter above, we were moving between different ways of
accounting for what goes on between us. The carefully structured agenda
initially proposed was a highly systematic account of how we get to grips
with ourselves and the world of human action as a logical 'problem' to be
solved. It is hard to argue against any element of the proposed plan – it is
perfectly logical, relentlessly so, I would say. Everyone knows that life
isn't quite like this, so implementing this idealized plan requires
engaging someone who might be able to help the group navigate the
murky shoals of 'charged' discussion so that it stays 'on track'.

Yet, in the midst of a conversation that constructed how we would work
together in a certain way, it was also possible for me to speak into
another, more improvisatory way of approaching how we might go on
together. We have much practical knowledge and skill relating to the
everyday art of 'going on together', knowledge that we create and use
from within the conduct of our communicative activity. People had a
sense of what I meant because of our mutual ongoing experience of the
disorderly way order arises and dissolves and reconfigures in human
affairs, a process we are never on top of or ahead of despite our
inescapable attempts to be so. It is as though our capacity for self-
conscious reflection gives us delusions of omniscience and omnipotence.
Our sophisticated capacity for observing our own participation tempts us
to think we can grasp the whole picture and manage its dynamics to suit
our well- or ill-meaning ends.

Most of what managers, leaders, consultants, and facilitators are asked to do
is 'to get ahead of the game', 'to be on top of the mess', 'to manage the
process', 'to set the boundaries', 'to delve beneath the surface to change the
deep structure'. It would seem that we want to think of ourselves anywhere
other than where we are, in the flow of our live engagement, sustaining and
transforming the patterning that simultaneously enables and constrains our
movement into the future. Because we don't seem to have a way to think
and talk about what we are doing in this reciprocal engagement, we have
become accustomed to a particular kind of systematic practice that is meant
to help us do this. Here is another example.

Not long ago I was invited to join a kind of international think-tank
sponsored in part by business, in part by policy units in government and

in part by educational institutions. The project was envisioned to last over two years to explore and articulate approaches to the emerging complex issues of today's world that might guide policy making. Some twenty-five people, academics, activists, scientists and psychologists among others, gathered for the first time in the evening for a three-day meeting. There was a brief welcome by the main business sponsor and the person leading the initiative. Then the facilitator stood up and introduced himself and explained the intended style and process of the next few days. He said that he considered that the role of a facilitator was to help what was trying to happen to happen and then get out of the way. Here is another interesting formulation of what it might mean to facilitate or enable. What did this turn out to mean in practice?

He pointed out the carefully designed setting that had been created for the meeting, including various technological aids that he suggested we would do well to familiarize ourselves with now so that we would be able to use them later. First he invited us to approach the terminals placed round the room and type in a comment about the start of the meeting – any comment would do – and then press the enter key. Immediately the screen would display all the other comments that had been entered so far and we could type in a response to any one and, by pressing the key, we could see all the responses. There was a noticeable reluctance to start this activity. Some people typed in a sentence or two, with others looking over their shoulders, but soon people drifted back to their seats.

The facilitator then suggested that we familiarize ourselves with another aid. He gave us all something akin to a mobile phone with a small keypad and told us it was a voting machine. He suggested that it would be very interesting to know about the connections between people in the group as we came together for the first time. A slide flashed up on the wall asking whether we already knew one, two, up to five or more than five people in the group. We were asked to press the appropriate key to indicate our choice of answer. Within a few seconds a bar chart of our responses appeared on the wall. The bar chart told us now that most people in the room knew two others before coming. But who knew who and how and what kind of bearing might that history have for us? At this point someone pointed out that the total number of responses on the chart did not match the total number present. Were some of the voting machines faulty or were some people not responding? We tried again with a similar result. The facilitator promised to check the machines. I imagined some feelings of disappointment as he continued as though what was happening was not what he had hoped might flow from these early activities.

There seemed to me to be a restlessness among those in the room. The odd thing was that the technological aids to our work were doing the opposite of aiding us. I am not making a point about technology as such, but about how the process of enabling was being approached. The machines proliferated messages and statistics in the midst of activities that did little to help us make meaningful connection. The computer screens had flashed up a few dozen messages in a way that confused the sense of who was responding to who about what. The complex temporal and spatial web of human responsive relating was addled so we were struggling with the creative process of constructing the possible significance of our presence here together.

An hour had passed before the facilitator suggested people introduce themselves to one another. He proposed a way we might do this as a start although we were free, of course, to choose any other way. I was struck by the sense that we needed a format for doing this to start us off, as though otherwise we might be at a loss how to begin to engage one another and it would be better to have something to fall back on.

The four corners of the room had been labelled with the four topics of the project and around each corner pieces of paper were stuck on the walls each carrying a few sentences. I realized by recognizing some of my own phrases that these were taken from material we had sent in before the meeting in response to a series of questions. The sentences were not attributed and I noticed that two remarks of mine that had followed one after the other had been pasted at different corners. Again I thought how odd this process was, distributing snippets disconnected from one another and from the author and from the question the author was responding to in the first place.

After introducing ourselves to one another we were asked to choose one of the corners of the room and to discuss our first thoughts with the group that convened there. Again it was assumed that the open space of exploring how we might begin together was just too anxiety-provoking or time-wasting to contemplate. A large board at each corner was marked out with an identical grid for us to fill in. The headings were prompts like: key issues under this topic, positive trends, negative evidence, aspirations for our work in this area, and so on. Again the facilitator assured us that this was just a starting point for the discussion and just a useful way of feeding back to the whole meeting. In the group I joined we ignored the board and then tried to fit our discussion to its constraints, or stretch the constraints to incorporate aspects of our discussion. As someone from each group 'reported back', the presenters followed the format of the grid. I listened to the person from my group give a fluent performance, linking up the words scrawled on the board brilliantly. I thought how well schooled we all are in this kind of process and how little of the tentative exploratory conversation we had just participated in was actually conveyed.

It was an enormous relief to go to dinner where the noise level was high, as many highly varied conversations worked in a disorderly way to start fashioning the links and associations between people. We were evolving the sense of the reciprocal relations between our gathering selves and the endeavour we were gathering for. Despite the facilitator repeating his wish to enable what was trying to happen and to 'get out of the way', something about how we were approaching the need to organize ourselves seemed to me strangely heavy-handed.

The legacy of process consultation and organization development

It seems to me that the profession of organization development and process consultation has ossified in ways that have become more inhibiting than enabling. What is this legacy that invites us to understand human processes in particular ways? We could look back at some of the classic and influential texts in the field, such as those written by Edgar Schein in the 1970s and 1980s. In his volumes on Process Consultation (1987, 1988) Schein writes about organizations in terms of networks of people and the various processes of interaction between them. Schein's stated intention is to analyse major human processes, such as communication or decision-making or leadership, and highlight what process consultants, whether as hired help or employed managers, would observe about such processes and what they might do about what they observe, that is, how they might intervene (1988: 13). The importance of human processes is understood thus: the network of positions and roles that define the formal, or designed, organizational structure is occupied idiosyncratically by individual people who put their own personality into getting the job done and who relate to others in their own unique way.

> These processes of relating to others have a decisive influence on outcomes and must themselves become objects of diagnosis and intervention if any organisation improvement is to occur.
> Paradoxically, some processes recur with such regularity that they become virtually part of the structure. . . . Structured processes (i.e.

observed regularities of behaviour) are very much the domain of the process consultant.

(ibid.: 17)

The expertise of process consultation is 'a good deal of knowledge of what to look for, how to look at it, how to interpret it, and what to do about it' (ibid.: 19).

As will become clear, Schein's idea of process and of participation are very different from mine. He talks about his work in terms of sitting in with people at various meetings. 'Not only have I observed my own communication with the client so far, but I can now observe how different members in the client organisation communicate with each other' (ibid.: 21). Schein's analysis of patterns depends on observing in terms of the regularities of behaviour of the different individuals present, including himself, and the way those regularities impact others in ways that also produce regularities of behaviour between them. In other words, he is observing what is stable and repetitive in the way people relate. He explains his practice in terms of his experience in identifying these patterns, bringing them to the attention of clients in a timely fashion and, with them, diagnosing their consequences for good or ill. Collaboratively he then helps people to institute patterns that they consider more useful. Thus the process consultant intervenes, and helps clients themselves to learn to intervene, in their own stabilized patterns in order to establish new ones. Schein's practice is that of a participant-observer. What is never questioned in his work is this account of how change occurs in patterns of relating. On the one hand he encourages reflection on the patterning that emerges over time in human relating, a patterning that is self-organizing; that is, a patterning that cannot be understood as intended by any single person or group. On the other hand he suggests that people can introduce new patterns that they do intend. The explanation for past patterns is different from the explanation for future patterns. At no time is there any indication in his writing that there is any contradiction in this. We participate, we pause, we observe and assess ourselves retrospectively, we make adjustments and we continue. The assumption is that in the process of reflection we can learn to design with increasing self-consciousness the patterns that it will prove useful to find ourselves in next time we pause to reflect. This is largely how collective learning is understood in organizations.

No wonder facilitators, consultants and managers informed by this tradition work as if they must propose well-designed patterns for all interaction in advance of interacting, as though that is what being enabling entails. Thus they fill the looming openness of the future with exercises, frameworks, structured agendas, matrices and categories as though, without them, there will not be a useful structuring of interaction. However, as this need to design the form of communication is apparent on the one hand, on the other hand the sense that unwanted patterns will continue to arise remains. Thus there is an ongoing need for process facilitation to keep things on track. This account of change in patterns remains within the cybernetic tradition of using feedback to keep a system from drifting off course.

So how might we begin to think differently about the way the patterning of human interaction patterns further patterning of human interaction? This is a book about the way we humans organize ourselves conversationally. The title, *Changing Conversations in Organizations*, is intended in several senses. I want to suggest a change in the way we often think of the part conversation plays in organizational life. We currently take it for granted as a background to more important activities through which we design and manage our organizations, as though conversation is carrying or transmitting the thing we should be focusing our attention on. Instead, this book will work with the assumption that the activity of conversation itself is the key process through which forms of organizing are dynamically sustained and changed. Our habits of thought and speech tend to blind us to the sheer flowing ubiquity of the communicative dance in which we are all engaged. Instead we focus mainly on the tangible products of conversation – the organizational designs, performance profiles, business models, strategic frameworks, action plans, lists and categories with which we seek to grasp the reified complexities of organizational life and render them 'manageable'. We spend much time extracting and generalizing from our lived experience and then trying to apply the abstractions as templates for shaping the future *as though we uncritically believe that this is how our future comes to have shape.* How often have you found yourself in meetings where 'tangible outputs', 'concrete results' and 'solid outcomes' is a constant pressure and concern? Without this way of thinking we fear that we will be literally 'at sea', awash in formless transience, without a rudder. Must it be so? On the contrary, this book will continue the argument of this entire series in suggesting that this fear is a consequence of a way of thinking that has become habitual in corporate and institutional life. We seem to lack a capacity to articulate the nature of our participation in the activities which give evolving form to our organizational experience.

Conversing as organizing, organizing as conversing

We think about 'an organization' as something that has an existence separate from our own activity, even though often we are uneasily aware that it is not so. The phrase 'in Organizations' in the title of this book is a further concession to the habit. In fact, I will not be writing about conversations that take place 'in' an organization, but about *conversing as organizing*. I will be describing and illustrating conversation as a process of communicative action which has the intrinsic capacity to pattern itself. No single individual or group has control over the forms that emerge, yet between us we are continuously shaping and being shaped by those forms from within the flow of our responsive relating.

I also want to notice a shift in the form and character of conversations that occur when people meet to talk about strategy, change, organization, culture and so on at meetings of one sort or another. Organizational meetings have acquired peculiarly unhelpful constraints on the mode of engagement that is judged effective and productive, even though, in most organizations I work with, people's frustration with meetings nearly always runs high. Again the way this frustration is understood tends to lead to a greater emphasis on managing meetings better, improving the pre-read, managing the agenda, managing the time, managing the discussion, polishing the presentations, capturing the outputs, identifying actions and managing the follow-up. Do people find this leads to more satisfying meetings? I do not think so. In this book I want to look at how we could approach the art of gathering and conversing in ways more conducive to the emergence of meaningful action, creative endeavour and differentiated identities.

Above all I want to propose that if organizing is understood essentially as a conversational process, an inescapably self-organizing process of participating in the spontaneous emergence of continuity and change, then we need a rather different way of thinking about any kind of organizational practice that focuses on change. The main focus of this book is practice, in other words the way we make meaning of the activities of any of us who may be explicitly charged with 'leading change', 'managing change', 'planning change' or 'facilitating change'. This book is not about systematic change methodologies based on abstract models of organization, rather it explores how we might make sense of our experiences of working with continuity and change day to day.

The question for us all is what do we think we are up to, how are we to account to ourselves and to others for the activities we initiate, support or discourage? How are we to explain what we do and don't do? How are we to think about our contribution? In other words, how are we to practise?

The value of 'just talking'

Let me continue by recounting an episode that occurred many years ago in the early 1990s when the issues that motivate me in writing this book first began to excite and trouble me.

I was sitting in the office of the Managing Director of a European Business Centre within a large global corporation. Imagine an airy, top-floor room with plate glass windows giving a far-reaching but dreary view of a London satellite conurbation. We sit, just the two of us, at a round conference table and are brought coffee by the MD's secretary in pale china cups. In this atmosphere of corporate privilege and power we are talking about the delicate issue of not knowing. What is this senior executive to do when he believes some kind of initiative is needed, but precisely why he thinks something is needed and what form that something should take eludes him?

We did not start here, of course. The meeting had begun crisply with the MD's intention to repeat the occasion of the previous year's strategic management meeting which had inaugurated the new European Business Centre. I had helped to design and facilitate this meeting of some eighty managers held in the Château of Chantilly in France. The MD tells me that, although business results have been satisfactory, the potential benefits of a more co-ordinated approach is not being realized in key accounts across Europe. The different businesses that have been brought together under the umbrella of the EBC remain, he feels, surprisingly intact, reducing communication and collaboration across related areas. This is despite implementing all the agreements made at the meeting that had inaugurated the new EBC, agreements that were intended to help cross-cultural and cross-functional communication. The MD shows me copies of the EBC newsletter produced monthly, to which all parts of the EBC send in progress reports and information. He also shows me the elaborate system of management briefing notes and feedback forms cascaded at regular intervals up and down the hierarchy. He describes the management tours he has twice conducted around all the sites in Europe, meeting and talking to groups of staff about business models, strategic plans and key priorities.

There is something very familiar to me about his concerns. He wants to act as a leader to improve the situation and is struggling to find ways to think about this. He has decided to organize another management meeting in the coming autumn to try to further rally the EBC and establish more effective patterns of working. He wants me to design and facilitate a meeting along similar lines to the last event (Where are we now? Where do we need to be? So how do we get there?), which he still sees as very successful.

I might once have accepted this proposal. Instead, the conversation has taken its currently more ruminative turn because I respond differently than I might once have done. I ask, who else is he talking with about the sense he is making of the situation? Who shares his concerns? What sense are others making? How has the idea of another large management meeting emerged? I ask how sure he feels about the value of such a meeting. I admit that, although I have often helped to create such meetings that are deemed to be very successful, I am left with nagging questions. Why do we always think that getting everyone together in one place at the same time to agree on a desired way forward is the best way to change things, especially when the nature of the change needed is subtle – a variation of the unending themes of better communication, better co-ordination, more initiative and more innovation? Why is it that these sessions always seem so successful at the time and yet fail to 'deliver' the kind of future people hope for? Does it make sense for the two of us to sit here designing outcomes and structures for a meeting to tackle something as pervasive and intangible as 'unrealized potential'?

As we explore these questions together, the clarity about exactly what we are doing and our respective roles in the conversation begins to dissolve. This is rather unsettling. No longer are we discussing a proposed future initiative, we are very much in the midst of things, talking about what kind of sense we can make of our experience. The quality of our communication changes. Unrehearsed expression replaces familiar and polished phrases. We surprise one another and even ourselves. We begin to speak about vague doubts each of us has, glimpses, half-formed ideas, intuitions that we clothe in words for the first time. We relate stories and anecdotes about previous experiences and conversations. We pay close attention to one another, listening carefully, yet the conversation makes unexpected jumps as each of us associates to what the other is saying.

We interrupt each other, interpret, misunderstand. The more we talk in this exploratory way, the less urgent the need to decide on an action becomes. The more we acknowledge that we do not know exactly what to do, the more slowly time seems to pass, or rather we become oblivious to it, as neither of us pushes for closure. In this kind of conversation the quality of risk and anticipation alerts my senses. I can recall the taste of coffee, the quality of light as the MD gazes out of the window at one point, the way the thick carpet absorbs sound and smells of some chemical cleaning fragrance. The outcome that emerges is our decision to continue this rather odd but intriguing conversation with an as yet unknown group of people in the EBC. This is not at all the kind of outcome either of us had in mind when we first started talking and, compared with a detailed plan for a strategic management meeting, scarcely seems worthy of two hours' discussion. We would have been hard put to summarize the conversation, yet it felt significant.

The MD agrees to write an open note to all his managers attempting to articulate his concerns and his sense that the potential of the new EBC is not being realized. Would a management meeting be useful? Who should attend and what form should it take? He will invite people to think and talk about his note and ask those who want to take an active part in taking the inquiry forward to contact his secretary, so that a meeting to discuss this further can be arranged in the next few weeks. I suggest that he does not set a limit on the numbers who might become involved nor indicate what part of the business or what level in the hierarchy they may come from. We would see what response the note produces. I imagine each person reading the note and making a different meaning. The response will not be random; the grouping that will meet will emerge out of a web of relationships and conversations in unique but relevant ways.

Eight people respond to the note and we meet in a conference room in early June. The MD welcomes the group, thanks people for responding to his memo and says he would like to leave people to discuss their views and will return in a couple of hours to hear their thoughts. I am not expecting him to go, but guess he is acting on the assumption that a fuller discussion may take place in his absence. The others look at me once the MD has left. We are all wondering how to start. There is an ambiguity about this gathering that disturbs routine behaviour and I wonder if the MD was relieved to leave us to it. I'm not sure how to begin either but I suggest that we hear what has prompted people to respond to the MD's note and what we all made of it. I am quite surprised by what happens next. Nearly everyone focuses immediately on the MD's suggestion for another large management meeting and voices doubts about it. How could such a meeting justify the costs, especially at the present time? What would be the outcomes? How could the merits of such a meeting be 'sold' to the rest of the organization? After about 45 minutes of this, there seems to be an atmosphere of gloom pervading the room. I ask whether the point of this meeting, as it turns out, is to inform the MD that his intuition that such a meeting would be useful is misplaced, or at least not shared by other managers. In this case, would it not be best to ask the MD to rejoin us to address this directly and look for other ways to approach his concerns? The gloom palpably intensifies. I ask whether people are reluctant to tell the MD that this is their collective view. Instead of an answer the discussion about why a meeting cannot be justified starts up again.

Puzzled, I try another tack. I ask them to put aside for a moment the need to justify and identify useful outputs from a proposed management meeting. How many of them feel there is important conversation to be had amongst their colleagues around Europe? One by one they all admit that on their own account, yes, they very much need such discussion, that was why they wanted to join this meeting today – a chance for some face to face time with colleagues before and after the official meeting.

So, I say carefully, the difficulty is that there is something unsatisfactory about the kind of discussion that goes on at a strategic management meeting? However, there is a kind of discussion that would be very useful, but they do not know how to justify this? Yes, said a Dutch manager, the coffee breaks are very useful, but the rest of the time is a poor return on the time invested. Suddenly the room becomes animated with anecdotes about this perennial problem, what is important is always discussed off-line.

I suggest that maybe the solution is a meeting designed as a prolonged coffee break. There is amusement, but I ask them what would happen if they take my remark as the seed of a serious idea. I speculate aloud about the self-organizing nature of ordinary conversation and wonder if this does not help to explain the effectiveness of coffee break discussions. Here no-one has overall control over who speaks to who about what, and yet patterns of response to the issues being addressed (or not!) in the formal meeting seem to emerge speedily.

Slowly, but with increasing interest, the group begins to play with this notion, the noise level rises considerably as the outline of an actionable proposal begins to take shape. When the MD returns a slightly more sober rendering of our discussions is summarized for him by the German manager present. Several others lend their support. The MD asks the Human Resources Manager for his views, who replies that he thinks that an unusual but interesting and workable idea has been generated during the meeting. 'Fine then,' says the MD, turning to me, 'I suggest you make a summary of the proposal and present it for discussion at the next Management Team meeting. If accepted I suggest this group becomes the design team for organizing these meetings.' I remember thinking that something about the spirit of what was happening was just about to be lost. I feared that it would be hard to stop my 'proposal' congealing into a familiar formulation. All my instincts were to keep this conversation moving. I ask the group if they would be willing each to jot down and send round their own understanding of our discussions, not just the outcome, but the nature of the shift in thinking that has taken place. Perhaps one or two of them could join the Management Team meeting and perhaps recreate the kind of shift that has emerged here? They agree happily to this and two managers offer to attend the meeting.

I left the meeting aware that whatever kind of work I was now engaged in, it certainly did not lead to a nice little package of agreed consulting days.

This conversation produced some interesting reflections by the managers. Here are a few examples taken from the emails they sent around. For most of them, English is not their mother-tongue.

> The transition to the EBC and what it means regarding managing our businesses has not yet been understood fully by the EBC management. And this will not be the last change – continuous change will be the normality in future, requiring new management styles. This creates a strong feeling of discomfort, which needs to be addressed. However the traditional rules of the corporation don't fit properly with this situation. Although we feel the need to meet and discuss, we can't justify the meeting with a proper agenda and expectations regarding the results. As we don't know exactly what the problem is, we can't solve it and this makes us feel uncomfortable again. To get out of this mess we have to be aware of this feeling of discomfort, use it as a driving force, don't try to replace it by an artificial harmony.
> The feeling only that a meeting is needed is justification enough to have one.

> This meeting must offer freedom instead of structure, it should have no other purpose than to find out where we are, what needs to be done, what will be our role in future, how do we manage a permanently changing situation.

We need to allow meetings which develop their own momentum and results – without driving them into a certain direction.

If there is facilitation and a certain structure this must be to help the meeting develop its own dynamic – not to hinder it.

These meetings should not be a follow-up of last year, but a first step to create a new management network in the EBC, which can cope with future challenges.

In the current day and age, and most likely also in the future, none of us working in organisations like this will have a quiet day again. This means that the managers need to feel comfortable in a constantly uncertain situation. This requires considerable resilience, getting to know one another, flexibility, ability to cope with people from different cultures and backgrounds. In order to arrive in such an atmosphere whereby the managers almost naturally would 'emerge' into a state of networking, we suggest a meeting/session whereby, contrary to company culture, very little would be organized beforehand, since in many of our meetings, most gets accomplished in the so-called coffee breaks or informal, non-organised get-togethers. We all generated quite a bit of excitement as to having such a session.

I was undecided and not committed to 'another' meeting either as a follow-up to last year or as a programme report on the EBC. However, if viewed as a method by which the EBC could grow in effectiveness by changing the way we communicate, then there is a benefit, and what's more – an immediate benefit.

Current 'regional' networks are being reformed, and EBCs are still forming networks across businesses and across regions/cultures/languages. An acceleration of this process would build the effectiveness of the EBC.

We need to develop skills of open discussion, covering sensitive issues that all too often get pushed aside by formal agendas. The format should be informal, using each other as sounding boards; increasing communication across businesses and functions as people share concerns. Not just the management but we should invite others who we feel are in a position to aid this process.

We must increase UNDERSTANDING of the EBC and how we can contribute to its business success. We need to enhance CONFIDENCE between managers. We need to learn to work in the 'TENSION' between the EBCs and Regions. We need lots of informal discussion to find and resolve issues.

We should have a meeting which is not a follow up to last year in Chantilly. No detailed agenda, the topics should be created through the interaction of the questions and intentions of the attendees. We should try to experience change. We felt very uncomfortable to have another Chantilly, but came to the conclusion that a more informal exchange of experiences and questions amongst self-organizing groups of managers would be of outstanding help and importance. It was very interesting to see how the group's opinion changed during the meeting and I personally felt very comfortable with the results.

Glimpsing another way of working

Looking back I now see these episodes as the beginning of a major shift in my practice as an organization development consultant. Coloured as it must be by my experiences over the last decade I would pick out certain themes in this story that intrigued me even at the time.

The invisibility of ordinary everyday conversation

These mature and experienced managers did not believe they could justify an explicit investment in the free-flow of open-ended conversation despite their conviction that this kind of conversation was precisely what they needed. It was not that they did not create opportunities to engage in such conversation, indeed they were adept at finding many ways to do this, but the dominant way of thinking about managerial effectiveness that they subscribed to did not render this legitimate. Their ways of thinking together meant they could not take an aspect of their experience seriously. In order to justify meeting, you had to know in advance exactly what the topics for discussion would be and what the outcomes of discussion should be. The more uncertain and ambiguous their situation, the more they wanted to meet and talk, yet the less legitimate the expense of doing this became. In order to justify the expense they felt bound to organize the kind of meeting that would not serve them. Catch 22!

Acting into the unknown

The managers' language was littered with references to continuous change, turmoil, discomfort, uncertainty and tensions. It was not obvious to them how to make sense of their situation, how to lead, how to act in particular circumstances, despite all the business models, strategic frameworks and key priorities that served as 'shared' representations of the organization's activities. It was not that they disagreed with these models, they found them useful, yet 'implementing' them was far from straightforward. They believed they needed a structure of thought which made sense of acting prior to taking action. They would often say things like, 'We know the problems, we can see the solutions, but we can't make the delivery mechanisms work.' They had excellent ways of discussing organizational strategy as idealized templates or blueprints for change, but they did not have ways of thinking about the unpredictability and ambiguity of their daily experience. It was not that they did not know themselves to be competent – they did work effectively in the midst of uncertainty, but it was as though they could not articulate what they were actually doing. In a way everything was clear and known and yet their experience was of acting into the unknown moment by moment. The world they inhabited and the world they presented to and discussed with each other seemed, at best, tenuously connected. There did not seem to be a way to talk about this officially other than to continue tinkering with models and implementation plans. Surely, they argued, either we know what we are doing or we don't.

Organizing the unorganizable

As they reflected on their experience of the way a certain open-ended quality of conversation generated purpose, meaning and innovation, the managers repeatedly referred to this as being non-organized, or not organized in advance, not designed, not managed, not driven. They referred to structures, leadership and facilitation which hindered a meeting from 'developing its own dynamic'. But at the same time, they experienced themselves individually as intentional, purposeful and strategic. Things were either organized or not organized. They were bemused at the prospect of trying to organize an unorganized meeting.

Wanting to capture knowledge

At the close of both my meeting with the MD and the subsequent meeting of the group of managers, a very satisfying sense of being able to go forward emerged. Yet, in both cases, most people were anxious that unless something – our ideas, our learning – was 'captured' in a report, a proposal, a summary, the satisfaction would prove illusory, would escape us, dissolve, cease to exist and, worst of all, that nothing further would happen. And yet my sense was that the conversations had changed things – our perceptions of ourselves in our situation – subtly but irrevocably. We could not easily undo these shifts, even if we wanted to.

The themes I am drawing attention to all involve paradox. What I began to glimpse as this and other assignments continued was that there could be a way of working, a form of organizational practice, that did not collapse or avoid these paradoxes but rendered them intelligible. I began an active search in the urgency of live assignments for a way of working with executives, managers and other consultants, that focused explicitly on all that I had begun to feel was ignored in the well-accepted approaches to organizational change.

A complexity approach to change

At the time of the assignment I describe here, I was excited by the potential of the so-called complexity sciences for offering fresh insights into the phenomena of organizing. A new language was appearing as scientists attempted to describe complex dynamics in which phenomena were no longer perceived as either ordered or disordered, either stable or unstable, either organized or disorganized, but could paradoxically be both *at the same time*. The concepts of self-organization and emergence offered the beginning of insight into the conundrums I outline above. It is the implications and possibilities of this idea that leads me to talk of a complexity approach to change.

This series is developing a particular way of thinking about self-organization as emergence in the world of human action. We draw analogies with some of the scientific work, and locate this in streams of thought in philosophy, psychology and sociology which seem to us to be pursuing similar insights. We develop a way of thinking which emphasizes the self-organizing patterning of communicative action in complex responsive processes of human relating (Stacey, Griffin and Shaw 2000; Stacey 2001). It is a way of thinking that invites us to stay in the movement of communicating, learning and organizing, to think from within our living participation in the evolution of forms of identity. Our blindness to the way we participate in fabricating the conversational realities of organizing is compounded by the difficulty we have in *thinking from within, in thinking as participants, in thinking in process terms,* above all, *in thinking paradoxically.*

Another way of thinking about the issues raised by our participation, our interdependence and our contextual embeddedness are tackled in recent developments in systems thinking, particularly second-order cybernetics, soft systems methodologies and living systems theory. In this series, we have argued that to think systemically usually means to deal with the paradoxes of human organizing by thinking in terms of *both/and* complementarities. This is a powerful advance over thinking in terms of simple either/or dichotomies, but it leads us to think about the conundrum of our capacity for self-conscious reflection in particular ways. This series explores a different way of thinking that stays in the tension of paradox as the movement of the sense-making process itself.

There are different complexity approaches to change, which can seem at first confusingly similar because they all bring a new attention to conversation, participation and the way we organize and are organized as we communicate. One aim of this book is to explore how this new emphasis on complexity and conversation plays out differently in practice. I will explore the difference between a systemic change practice as advocated by the majority of influential writers and practitioners in the field of organizational change and a participative practice that understands itself without recourse to systems thought. I will ask whether the differences matter and how and to whom?

In Chapters 2 to 5 I will describe my practice by telling stories that echo repeatedly the themes of complexity and emergence while emphasizing different aspects (the names of people and places are often changed). The way each story or practice narrative is told illustrates again and again the kind of sense-making at work, as I work, and as I speak about the work I do. I will relate my experiences of organizational change without seeking to extract universally applicable prescriptions. On the contrary, my intention is to convey an appreciation of 'form' from within the narratives. They are intended to be instructive accounts. As you read the stories I hope you will notice how I am asking you to think about organizational change, how I am encouraging you to shift your attention to particular aspects of your experience of organizational life. I will also keep asking myself reflexive questions: How am I thinking about what is going on? How am I making sense of my own and other's participation?

Chapters 6 and 7 act as a counterpoint to the earlier chapters by looking first at the legacy of organizational development and then at the approaches of other organizational practitioners who embrace conversation and participation as keys to their work. How do they describe, illustrate and account for their practice? I will look particularly at the recent interest in concepts such as Open Space Technology, Future Search conferencing, the Learning Organization, Dialogue, and Communities of Practice. How do these practitioners appear to be thinking about what they are doing? Where do we share similar concerns and where do our interests diverge?

2 Making sense of gathering and gathering to make sense

- 'Changing the culture' at Broadstone
- Making sense of this story: interviewing myself
- 'Changing the culture' at Ferrovia
- Making sense of this story: continuing the interview

'Changing the culture' at Broadstone

This story begins with a phone call from John. He has not met me before but he is ringing on the suggestion of Clare, a colleague. A key project leader employed on a contract basis has left the organization, saying he has become terminally frustrated with the culture of Broadstone, he cannot get anything done, innovation is impossible, he feels baulked at every turn. This has touched a nerve with John, the Human Resources manager at the UK site of a telecommunications company which has recently grown with a number of international acquisitions. 'We're being told to become more global and more innovative but it feels like treacle here.' Could he and I meet to discuss 'how to change the culture'?

I say I would be happy to come to talk with him and suggest we include others in the meeting so that we can discuss what people are making of what has happened. At first John hesitates; wouldn't it be better for us to meet first before involving anyone else, so that he can brief me and we can sketch out an approach? I ask what makes him hesitate about going straight into a more inclusive conversation that would engage more viewpoints, interest and ideas about what is going on and what needs to change? There is a pause, and I say that I am increasingly doubtful about 'culture change' programmes in situations like this. Yes, says John, we've already had countless change programmes . . . I can sense a difference in his voice, he sounds less 'business-like', less rehearsed. So

I add that, of course, the trouble is that culture can't be changed by making edicts and plans in the way we seem to hope. He half laughs. So what does he think of my suggestion? He begins to consider it: who would it be best to invite? What should he announce as the purpose of the meeting? I ask him who is already involved, who he is already talking with, who might be interested in such a conversation? What if he did not try to compose an invitation but instead sounded out a number of people, tried to engage their curiosity. John begins musing about various people he would like to invite to such a conversation and what he might say. We agree a date and I leave it to John to gather whatever grouping can free the time to join us. He asks about numbers and I tell him that exact numbers are less important than his own sense of the existing connections he wants to draw on and new ones he wants to make. Just before the conversation ends I say that we could think of the gathering and the conversation we would have as itself contributing to change, as the start of working together. Does that make sense to him? Yes, he says, it does actually, he likes it.

On the day of our meeting I leave home early for the wretched drive around the London orbital motorway to Broadstone. As I approach I realize that I have failed to ascertain exactly where the site is located, so I call John on my mobile, but his answer machine responds. I leave a message to say I am about half an hour away and will call reception to get precise directions.

I find the site in a number of buildings arranged around a small lake on an unprepossessing industrial estate just outside the town centre. Parking the car is difficult, the site car parks are overcrowded. I wait in reception for John who comes down the stairs to greet me looking a bit flustered:

> You didn't get my message then? I left a message on your office answer machine first thing this morning to say that I heard late yesterday that a few key people that I wanted to attend this meeting couldn't make it, so I called to cancel and to ask you for an alternative date. But then I got your message this morning and realized you were coming anyway, so in the spirit of our last conversation I went out and spoke to various people in the office and phoned a couple of others so I have convened a group. It isn't the one I had in mind, it's more ad hoc, but maybe that doesn't matter?

He looks inquiringly for my reaction and I smile, genuinely delighted that he has responded in this way to the unexpected developments, amplifying the unpredictability of the situation rather than playing safe.

We convene in an enjoyably messy way, organizing coffees from the machine and squeezing into a small meeting room filled with far too much furniture so that the nine of us are pinned to the walls, struggling to get round each other to find a seat. The situation has a definite air of novelty and people seem to like that. John begins to tell the story so far and what has happened this morning to produce this gathering. He becomes more relaxed as he gets into the story and I take up in the same vein emphasizing the interweaving of intention and chance that has brought us together in this room – a group of people asking ourselves, why us? Who are we in this situation and what sense can we make of being here together?

I add to John's story my own history of involvement so far and it takes little encouragement for others in the room to join in. Putting together a story naturally involves explaining something about ourselves, so that introductions and scene-setting evolve together. Illustrations, asides, further bits of background, other names are introduced in the attempt to recount, and simultaneously account for, the incident of the project manager leaving. What had led up to this and why he might have left is constructed amongst us. Slowly the particular incident that started off the conversation is left behind. Other themes become stronger as people begin to talk about the changes taking place in the company, how they know of these changes, what conversations they have had about them and what connections they make with their daily experiences. Since the people in the room have diverse roles and positions and length of time with the organization, there is a lot of variety in the material introduced into the conversation and the sense being made of it. I participate in the conversation by bringing my own experiences of working with change in other organizations, so that my way of thinking and speaking is introduced concretely rather than in a general way. After a couple of hours the energy begins to subside and I say, 'Well this has been a very interesting conversation.' Others agree and John says, 'Where does this take us?' I look round and ask people what they think. What difference has it made to them to participate in this conversation and where might it lead?

A young woman software engineer who has only been with the company a fortnight says that she had thought that being a newcomer was the source of everything she was experiencing. Now she felt that, after all, she was very much in tune with what was going on and this conversation had made sense of many things so that she felt much more part of the company. Another man is a contractor in a similar position to the one who has resigned, and he says that this was one of the best conversations he has had for a while and that he feels similarly about the issues we discussed as the full-time employees. Another section manager says he feels more motivated than he has for a long time, that perhaps there is more sense in what has been happening than he had realized and this gives him a new sense of purpose and optimism. He says, 'I really think we should continue this conversation and involve others. It would help a lot if more people in my department had a better grasp of what is going on in the company.' This proposal is greeted with approval round the room and he turns to John and asks if he could organize another gathering. I suggest that perhaps John could find a bigger room but wouldn't the best thing be for everyone here to decide who else to invite to the next conversation and just let John know? That is agreed as the next step. What shall we say is the topic, the reason for gathering? We have covered so many things. Why not stick with my original question, says John: 'How do we change the culture?'

I stay on briefly to talk with John who is very pleased with the conversation and its outcome. We agree that we are working on the premise that this *is* how culture changes and I send him an email afterwards saying some more about how we might think together about what we are doing.

Making sense of this story: interviewing myself

Questioner: You are telling this as an example of approaching organizational change in a particular kind of way, so what do you think is particular about it? What is the story illustrating?

Responder: Before we start this, I want to say that this making further sense of the story I have told is a continuously evolving process. There isn't a list of points that exists separately from the story and which the story illustrates. Every time I think or talk about my experience I am recreating its meaning, so having this conversation continues to evolve the significance I find in my retelling of events. Both the narrative and this reflective conversation are elaborating a form of work.

Questioner: You mean that the stories you tell keep changing! Does that mean they are fictions?

Responder: It is not a question of fact or fiction, one true, one false. To narrate has its roots in the word 'gnarus' – to know. In narrating we create meaning by bringing things into relation, by making connections, by drawing attention in one way or another so as to create a pathway in time, a train of events. We use the narrative form all the time as we relate our lives to one another. This is a form of *poiesis*, the Greek root of the word poetry, which simply means 'making'. It is an everyday art form by which we make ourselves together. The interesting thing about meaning is that it is always relational, it is always emerging as we tell our stories and respond to one another.

Questioner: Wait a minute, surely there is an agreed core of material, the 'data' if you like, that does not evolve?

Responder: You mean things like the number of people at the meeting, the date we met, the length of the meeting, the room number that we met in? I am talking about the way my story creates meaning by drawing attention in certain ways rather than others, by emphasizing certain moments rather than others, by using certain forms of expression rather than others. All stories are rhetorical and more or less persuasive, but that does not mean that we can say anything we like. As I describe events in my professional life throughout this book, I am constructing narratives that change in emphasis as I go on thinking and speaking about them. I want to sustain relationships with all the people in these stories who are colleagues and clients and friends who must be able to resonate with my tellings. I have much freedom in the telling, as we all have, yet each time I am constrained by the need to stay connected with the evolving meaning making of others. And not just that. For me, a worthwhile telling does not simply reaffirm existing ideas, it must *enliven the senses* of speakers, hearers or readers, stirring us from the habits of familiar ways of drawing attention to awaken a fresh appreciation of our experience.

Questioner: Why are you saying this? Why do you think it's important?

Responder: What I am talking about here is the same process that I am highlighting in my description of the meeting at Broadstone. The same process of people having to weave their sense-making in with others was at work there. Discussing the significance of the contracted manager's leaving was a creative social act in which we were patterning the complex flow of organizational activity in which everyone is taking part. The kind of sense we could make was being mutually constrained because it was informed by our histories of relating. The patterning of conversation is creating continuity and yet, at the same time, the possibility for unexpected connections occur and this changes what becomes possible. It is this kind of art or craft that I want to pay attention to as critical for any practice of organizational change. The material we are working with is malleable but not infinitely so at any one time, the constraints we feel are very real.

Questioner: Does this lead to a particular methodology of working?

Responder: Not if we use the word 'methodology' to indicate a blueprint for action, an orderly arrangement of ideas, a systematic framework or recipe that we can literally spell out and follow. That is not what I mean. However, there may be method as in phrases like 'there is method in my madness'. This captures the sense of forms arising and dissolving without blueprint, something recognizable rather than exactly repeatable. When I talk about a complexity approach to change, I am drawing attention to a spontaneous artfulness at work in the self-organizing shaping of organizations and society at large in which we are all engaged. I am suggesting that we could approach the work of organizational change as improvisational ensemble work of a narrative, conversational nature, a serious form of play or drama with an evolving number of scenes and episodes in which we all create our parts with one another. This does not mean that business models, tools and plans are not valuable, but my focus is more on how we devise them and make use of them as important props in the drama.

Questioner: So let us go back over the story you told. It starts with a request to help with culture change in an organization . . .

Responder: Yes, that was John's opening gambit. As soon as he began talking this way about 'how to change the culture', I experienced a visceral reaction, a tightening of my muscles in a refusal of this kind of way of talking about culture as a thing to be changed. I know it is not a thing and I am sure it cannot be changed in the way I often hear managers speak. But I did not want to start an abstract discussion about 'culture', because that would perpetuate talking about 'it'.

Questioner: Yet you do report saying something like this quite explicitly to John.

Responder: Yes, but by then our conversation had shifted quite a lot. At first I just wanted to disturb the way our proposed meeting was settling into something habitual – client invites consultant to come and explain how they would approach a change project. I feel that kind of conversation like a trap closing in on both of us and I wanted to literally talk my way out of a familiar set of mutual responses. So I concentrated my attention more on the story John was telling me as background to his call, the particular incident of the contractor leaving and the importance he was attaching to this. I imagined the other conversations that must be taking place to locate this latest incident in people's ongoing construction of 'what's going on here'. So I asked about who else he was talking with and that led to the suggestion of a meeting with a group of people.

Questioner: Would you say that meeting with a group, rather than one individual, is an important part of your approach? I notice you often make this suggestion.

Responder: I don't think that is the important point in itself. That's the difference between methodology and method. It's more that I am thinking in terms of joining the conversations that are already taking place between people. I know that there are no real beginnings of change. There are just points we allocate to order our stories and for political purposes, just as I chose the phone call with John rather than any number of other possible starting points, each of which would have situated the story differently. We are always in the midst of a paradoxical process of continuity and change. I am trying to think 'in the middle', to participate in the evolving sense that is being made between people as they relate. And, of course, that was going on all the time as John and I talked on the phone, one to one.

Questioner: What do you mean?

Responder: That the meaning of what we were doing as we discussed our proposed first meeting was shifting as we talked. At first it was implicit in John's desire to meet and brief me before involving others, that we must know clearly what we are doing before each action step. He should meet me first, he should make sure I had all the background, we should design together a way forward so that we knew what a next meeting should achieve. Then we would have a clear rationale for inviting and briefing others and they would come with a sense of knowing what they were doing there and so on. As we talked I was trying to speak my way out of this pattern of understanding that we were recreating together and instead evoke one in which we might think of ourselves as finding out what we were about in the actual doing of it. What started as a 'briefing meeting' became briefly a 'joint diagnosis', then more of a 'sense-making gathering' and in the end I suggested this *was* the work of culture change.

Questioner: So you are shifting from one kind of rationale to another.

Responder: Yes from a thought before action, design before implementation, systematic, instrumental logic of organizing, towards a paradoxical kind of logic in which we see ourselves as participating in the self-organizing emergence of meaningful activity from within our disorderly open-ended responsiveness to one another.

Questioner: Is this not just a difference in learning style?

Responder: No, as you say that you are already accepting an abstract model of learning which has been developed from Kolb's (1984) original dialectical ideas. Often these refer to cycles with phases of 'experiencing', 'reflecting on experience', 'conceptualizing' and 'active experimenting'. People are then seen as having preferences for parts of this cycle more than others, each unique pattern being a learning style, but that is to miss that the model itself separates thought from action, reflection from experience, in order to think with a certain kind of logic. I believe people like these models because the world is immediately resolved into categories and types to be looked at from the outside. With all these models, ambiguity, uncertainty and paradox are removed in order to be able to think in a certain way, as a designer, as an engineer, as a technologist. I am interested in a logic that is always dissolving categories and staying in the tension of the paradoxes inevitably created by thinking within the movement of sense-making itself. In the movement of our everyday communicative activity, we are creating who we are and what we can do together within shifting constraints of a material, technological and social nature. This is not the way we usually describe what we are doing in organizations. The designer–engineer voice predominates. This has become the voice of professional people, people seeking to be instrumental in shaping the world according to their expressed intentions. I think we are coming to appreciate the limitations of this dominant way of thinking. It is becoming increasingly clear that simple control over the outcome of complex interaction is indeed illusory. In organizations, at least, there is little confidence that there are other ways of thinking about what we are doing together.

Questioner: So you are trying to legitimize other kinds of voices, other ways to think and speak?

Responder: Yes, I suppose all my attention from the beginning of the call was to respond to John in a way that did not continue the familiar, 'professional' patterning of our responses so that we could voice our experience differently. Rather than designing changes in something called the organization's 'culture', I wanted to encourage us to stay in the midst of playing our part in the ongoing shaping of our situation.

Questioner: Is this really different from just saying you are applying a different model?

Responder: I am not applying a systematic model of communication or of organization, although I am theorizing differently about the processes of organizing. I am shifting attention to different aspects of what might be happening. As John and I spoke, I was feeling more or less constrained as the kind of work we might do was actively being shaped between myself and John. I was influencing but not determining that evolving shape as we spoke, as was he. This is what I mean by working within our participation with others, as we are simultaneously shaped by and shape our conversations. Both John and I were intentional and, at the same time, the outcome of our conversation was emerging in an unplanned, unpredictable way, yet recognizable enough for us both to continue response by response.

Questioner: You reached a shared understanding by the end of the conversation?

Responder: I doubt that. I don't think we shared one understanding or one shared picture of our proposed meeting. Rather we felt able to go forward into something we did not need to over-specify in advance. We had developed enough confidence to improvise a next step.

Questioner: What made you so pleased about the mess up over your first meeting?

Responder: What do people often mean by a mess? That their plans have been disrupted and they need to go back to the drawing board to design order back into the situation. John's first reaction was to do that, to go back to recreate his original intention, but then he seems to have remembered something different about the 'spirit' in which I had suggested we perceive our work and he decided to improvise a different next step. At that point he no longer had a very clear idea about how the meeting 'should' develop and so, as we gathered, we were all improvising.

Questioner: Can such an uncertain and ambiguous situation really be productive? Doesn't it waste time?

Responder: When we improvise I think we are just experiencing more
sharply the essential uncertainty and potentiality that is always
inherent in our communicative action. We may notice subtle and
complex changes in body rhythms – quickened heart rate, more blood
flow at the skin surfaces, more oxygen and so on. Different people
might speak of this experience as anticipation or nerves or tension.
Depending on how people express themselves verbally and non-
verbally, and how they respond to each other, such sensations may
amplify into feelings of excitement, fearfulness, humour, anxiety,
warmth or irritation. At the very least, people often say something
about feeling lively or enlivened and certainly engaged. I am interested
in conversations in which participants experience a heightened but not
debilitating sense of uncertainty and ambiguity, in which a
spontaneous, less rehearsed participation becomes more likely.

Conventionally meetings in organizations are carefully orchestrated to
do the exact opposite; they are over-specified in advance, so that the
experience of constructing the future together in interaction, a process
which is still taking place, is muted and the likelihood of people
constructing the familiar together is greater. Outcomes, procedures for
working together, agendas, roles to be taken up by those present, form
of contribution, pre-prepared slide presentations, room layout, all
conspire to reduce the experience of uncertainty. The experience of
acting into the known is engineered – participants know what they are
here for, know what they should do and know what the outcome
should be. There may be a place for this when sustaining what
currently exists is being sought. In the situations I describe, the
experience of acting into the unknown is enhanced. Even so, we are
not starting with a blank sheet. Everyone is 'making sense' with others
of their participation and that sense has to make connections with the
past and the possible future. The under-specification increases the
experience of diversity and multiplicity, disturbing routinized
responses and increasing the potential for novelty.

Questioner: What part did you play? Were you facilitating the meeting?

Responder: If by facilitating you mean participating as fully and
responsively as I can in the conversation, voicing my opinions,
associations and ideas along with everyone else, then yes.

Questioner: But surely that is what everyone is doing! Why engage you?

Responder: Yes, exactly. But I have slowly developed a practical feel for
the process of shaping and patterning in communication as I

participate. I have a keen sense of the move towards and away from agreement, of shifts in power difference, the development and collapse of tensions, the variations in engagement, the different qualities of silence, the rhetorical ploys, the repetition of familiar turns of phrase or image, the glimpsing and losing of possibility, the ebb and flow of feeling tone, the dance of mutual constraint. I try to play a part in this by participating in the conversation in a way that helps to hold open the interplay of sense-making rather longer than would occur in my absence, to hold open the experience of not-knowing. In organizational settings the pressure for closure can seem enormous. I think I have learned how to help people sustain an open-ended exploration and begin to notice the way they are generating useful ways of knowing and acting together as they do so. I try to shift people's perspective to see that organizational change *is* this process rather than an end product of it. I would say it is a particular form of facilitative leadership and I work with several people in senior positions of authority who are increasingly interested in developing their capacity to take up this potential in organizational settings.

Questioner: But what makes you think this whole episode was useful? What was the result? What changed?

Responder: At this first meeting we had gathered a grouping that had no formal existence or purpose in the organization but which began to intensify a process of actively questioning what was happening and their own part in this. The section manager spoke about generating a new sense of purpose and wanting others in his department to get a better grasp of what was going on in the company. I wanted to point out to him that the sense and purpose were not 'there' to be discovered. Instead we had created them together in the act of conversing. By the end of that first meeting we had begun to tap a web of existing and potential relationships giving rise to a train of events which developed an increasingly focused inquiry into patterns of working at Broadstone. We did not try to analyse the culture, instead we began to discuss people's own experience of influencing their situation – what kind of changes they tried to initiate, what happened in the process and how they could try other approaches, particularly being more active in engaging other relevant parties. This involved very concrete efforts from changing aspects of the working environment to developing ways of creating very different kinds of databases for enabling contact between people in an organization where it was hard to know what others were doing. Wherever people came up against the hurdle of things being 'not possible' our strategy was to invite further conversation between those generating this form of mutual constraint to see how this might loosen or shift. In this way, our activity touched the networks of formal and informal power relations that patterned the organization. I would say that this disturbance of repetitive patterns that allows new ones to emerge is what organizational change is all about. In fact, this particular initiative at Broadstone ran out of steam as we failed to keep alive the tentative connections we began to forge between sources of authority at Broadstone and at headquarters. In addition, the company was badly affected by the problems besetting the whole telecommunications industry bidding for very expensive broad band licences. Other interactions were having their own unexpected consequences. Waves of cost-cutting disrupted the relationships we had fostered as people were made redundant, left or failed to have their contracts renewed.

Questioner: Perhaps I need another example.

Responder: This next story is taken from a consulting assignment with the spin off business of a large global manufacturing and sales corporation. The question there too had been, 'How do we change our culture?' This was perceived as a challenge for a new organization with all the same people working in the same businesses but no longer under the umbrella of the parent company. Their question was: how do we escape our own traditions? The episodes I describe took place some months into the assignment.

'Changing the culture' at Ferrovia

Over lunch at a meeting in the UK with the Technical Services Team, I mention that I have been visiting Ferrovia, the Italian chemicals plant that is now the main manufacturing site for the new company. Before the spin-off, it had been one of many factories and research labs around Europe, viewed with some frustration as an incorrigible thorn in the flesh of all 'change programmes'. People had often told me how penetrating below the skin of the plant was nigh impossible for outsiders, they were courteously welcomed and subtly held at bay. Vice-presidents from the US, business heads chasing improvements in quality or delivery times, colleagues wanting information on research projects, all retired bemused, unable to pierce the life of the plant nestling in its valley, the main employment for generations of local people. Things had worked well enough to be tolerated, but now that Ferrovia has become the main manufacturing and research site for the new spin-off company in Europe, concern has increased.

When I ask at the lunch table about people's experiences at Ferrovia there is the usual pessimism about the plant, but one or two say that there are a few signs of change, some people are much more open and collaborative. Who? In what kind of circumstances? I write down the names of people and projects on a paper napkin. Over coffee I join another group and ask them about working at Ferrovia. Over the next couple of weeks as I work with different groups at meetings around Europe, I ask people about their experiences of collaboration with colleagues at the plant and slowly add to my list.

One name is mentioned repeatedly: Alessandro, a young manager in the technical support area of Medical Imaging. It seems to me that he is a node in a dense web of relationships inside and beyond the plant. One morning in early September I call him. I ask if he knows who I am, if he remembers the message that was sent out a couple of months ago introducing my colleague, Douglas Griffin, and myself as consultants working to 'help develop the new company'? He does not. I explain briefly about the kind of work Doug and I are doing, not initiating change programmes but joining various groupings of people who formally or informally are helping to evolve the working patterns of the new company. I tell him that his name keeps cropping up in my conversations with people around Europe as someone who is 'getting it' at the plant, whatever 'getting it' might mean. I read out the list of names I have. He is interested. Yes, he can understand why I might have many of these names – the majority have experience outside of the plant, have worked in the US and other parts of the company in Europe, they have a broader range of relationships. But he feels some important names are missing from my list. I ask if he thinks he could convene an informal gathering of any of these people who would be interested in talking with us about how Ferrovia is evolving. Yes, he says he will do it. Could I write a brief note to help him? I write a few paragraphs and fax them to Italy:

> We know that a different culture cannot be announced or imposed by an act of will. 'Culture' develops itself day by day in the practical interaction of doing business in the new circumstances. Sometimes people believe that Ferrovia is less affected than other parts of the company by the spin-off and so feels less impetus for change. At the same time others already see significant shifts in the way people are thinking and working at the plant. They talk of people beginning to

'get it'. What might this mean? Our invitation is to ask a group of you
to help us explore and elaborate what this might all be about.

During August, Stefano, in charge of management development at the
plant, also contacts Doug and myself in a more formal capacity. He is
preparing a training and development plan for the following year as part
of encouraging further change at the plant and it has been suggested to
him by his counterpart in the UK that he talk this over with us.

This provides an official reason for going to Italy again and September
finds us both with ten Italians in a room in the Medical Imaging Building
at Ferrovia. This is one of the few new buildings on the site, light,
colourful with a very different atmosphere compared with the wood
panelled solemnity of the Dirigenti building or the dark mazes of the
other office buildings. Those gathered round the table include
Alessandro, Franco, the youngest manager on the site committee, and one
of the people I have met on Cesare's Quality project (see later, p. 58) and
several people I have never met. Everyone introduces themselves,
although the Italians mostly know of one another despite working in
many different parts of the plant. Alessandro mentions the names of
several others who were very interested in joining this discussion, but are
unable to attend. There seems to be no expectation that we will try to
define any goals or outcomes for our meeting. I realize that Alessandro
has conveyed that this is a chance for a very open-ended exploration. We
find ourselves flowing between English and Italian so that any part of the
conversation is always hard to grasp in detail by at least some of us
present. We attempt no structured questioning. Doug and I talk about our
experiences at the plant so far and they talk about theirs. The
conversation flows irregularly, from one association to another, one story
to another. We linger for some time on the subject of phones. It is very
significant to these people that access to direct dial international lines is
available only to the upper echelons of management. There is frustration
that people at their level could not just pick up a phone and call others
anywhere else in Europe or the US without going through the
switchboard. The brainstorming 'change' sessions recently introduced at
the plant have thrown this up very early on and it is felt that the
managerial response has been slow. Franco insists that this had been
taken seriously and an updated system is being installed.

Linked with this sense of narrow channels of communication is a long
discussion about the poor perception of the plant in the rest of the
company. What is the pattern of these perceptions? How do they seem to

arise? Why do they seem so long-lived and difficult to shift? We tell stories of our experience of how difficult it is for outsiders to penetrate beyond the official managerial welcome of the plant. They tell stories of their experience of how few people ever try to make more direct connections or to spend more time here. So much is actually happening and changing in their daily experience, but they feel this is not apparent to enough people. They believe that a mutual feeling of collaboration is rare and this has led to the identification of themselves as 'getting it', because they have been part of such collaborative endeavours.

The meeting started at 10 a.m. and it is now 11.40 a.m. I know the Italians tend to lunch early. Someone suggests a coffee. We troop down to the basement. The coffee machines in Ferrovia seem all to be located in the basements. We continue talking. I feel some tension rising in me. What if nothing apparently comes of this discussion? It feels rich. There is real flow of interest in the subjects that emerge. Is that enough? I know also that no stronger shape can be forced if it is not emerging of its own accord. We return to the room a little after 12.15 p.m. We all sit down again. No one seems particularly keen to leave. Does everyone have the same sense as I do, I wonder to myself, that we are seeking a form to talk and act into? The idea we keep returning to is still the perception of Ferrovia as fatally unable to change. I recap that what is unique about the group that has gathered in the room today is that this is part of a network that crosses the plant areas and is also linked to people in other parts of the company. Could we intensify that? Could they imagine taking the initiative to use their contacts to invite some unusual groups of people to the plant, to take part in some open-ended meetings around issues that were scarcely yet formed? Who would they want to ask? What would they want to talk about? As I speak I get up and start drawing circles, some small and some large and links between them as I start to imagine possible conversations.

Alessandro picks this up immediately and I am convinced that intuitively he too was looking for what might be amplified in our discussion, not worrying exactly where it is going. He begins to talk about who he would love to have a conversation with about the way the strategy in Medical Imaging is forming. I interrupt and hand him the pen. 'Sketch out for us the groupings you have in mind. Who do you want to bring together, what are the relationships you feel are there, what is the potential you see?' He begins to talk and draw excitedly. After a little while I ask if this is beginning to give other people ideas about conversations they would like to convene. I suggest that we take some time for people to develop their thoughts alone or in a small group. I am aware that I am shifting in the kinds of suggestions I make as more structure and urgency is emerging. Very quickly the group organizes itself into two pairs and a foursome, while Alessandro and one other each works alone.

The clock ticks round to well past one o'clock. I point out the time. Is this OK? Does anyone need to go? Everyone wants to stay, lunch is unimportant. Doug and I look at one another in mute surprise and delight. The excitement in the room is tangible. Something has taken off! The groupings begin to share their ideas with one another. By now a lot of this is in Italian and Doug and I have only a rough idea of exactly what each proposal is about, but we know this does not matter. The key question is whether or not this energy will build up into further action or dribble away once we have all left the room. 'Would anything stop you just doing this?' we ask. 'Would you take this conversation seriously and start talking with people to see if you can bring these conversations about? We will join and support you in whatever way we can.'

Making sense of this story: continuing the interview

Questioner: You seem to have picked out a key group of informal influencers to gather together to initiate further change at the plant.

Responder: Be careful. You are looking at the process of how informal leadership emerges and then ascribing this as something 'in' the individuals who came together. You are following the way, in organizations, we focus our attention on the individuals themselves. It is assumed that there are special people who have special talents that warrant further development and grooming. I am paying attention to the way influence arises in webs of relationships in particular contexts and that it is the process of relating itself that I am attending to. It may look as though this gathering seems to depend on identifying certain named individuals. But these individuals have significance in the context of their ongoing relationships. They are not important because of some intrinsic capacity that can be separated from the communicative interaction in which that significance arises, *even though they may indeed be developing particular capabilities through their history of relating.* So I am not just identifying informal influencers but participating in the process by which leadership emerges.

Questioner: Both the gatherings you describe, at Broadstone and at Ferrovia, have a similar messy quality. People seem to be sitting down for a conversation with a very vague sense of why they are there or what they are trying to do, yet, surprisingly, people seem motivated to work together in this setting.

Responder: I don't think it is surprising. The urgent need to make sense of their involvement stimulates people's engagement. In this case the idea of 'getting it' was a strong stimulus. Getting what? Everyone has the opportunity to contribute on the basis of their own diverse interests, preoccupations and concerns. We all had to work to include ourselves in a very loose 'project' of inquiry that started to organize itself as the conversation developed.

Questioner: Does this bear some relation to the popular use of focus-groups?

Responder: No, it is the antithesis of focus groups. This involves a very clear formulation of an inquiry and the special invitation of a representative sample of stakeholders who are deemed to have an interest in the outcome of the inquiry. The idea is to canvass opinion to be used by those setting up the focus groups. The form of gathering I am describing here is quite different. There is no attempt to be representative or fair or to set agreed criteria for involvement. The gathering is not consultative, it is active. There are multiple sources of invitation as people suggest others and the process of inclusion and exclusion emerges in a history of connection and relationship in a self-organizing way. This raises its own questions of ethics and the need to stay alert to the emerging meaning of such inevitable including–excluding processes. Also, as I have said, there is ambiguity rather than focus in the formulation of the inquiry, which I consider necessary rather than detrimental. The point is to work with the potential for change, finding ways of convening forums which tap people's interests, enthusiasms or frustrations and which demand an intensive interaction to create meaningful forms of activity which 'move things on'.

Questioner: You do not seem to discuss any 'ground rules' for making the most of these gatherings or discuss any kind of objectives, you just seem to start.

Responder: Yes, I am not trying to set up a special kind of interaction. These discussions have an 'everyday quality' – they are messy, branching, meandering, associative and engaging. They are similar to the mode people value and recognize in many informal kinds of conversation. They include formulating and making reference to proposals, analyses and frameworks. They involve jargon, speculation, anecdotes and personal revelation. They are shot through with feeling tone and bodily sensation with which we are all resonating and responding to in different ways. It is a very active, searching, exploratory form of communication in which the way the future is under perpetual construction is more than usually evident to us all. In a way, the participants are constructing an emergent story, or more accurately a complex web of stories in which they themselves and the activities in which they are engaged are evolving as meaning shifts and evolves. That evolution is self-organizing, every participant plays an important part, yet, while no-one is single-handedly in control of the evolution, the evolution is not out of control either.

The kind of storytelling I am alluding to is not that of completed tales but narrative-in-the-making. Rather than stating aims, objectives, outcomes, roles as abstract generalities, people use a narrative mode. The starting point is often 'the story so far'. Someone recounts and at the same time accounts for or justifies, the way they make sense of events and their own participation. The point in the past which they chose to start their narrative and the path they construct to bring them to the present and to point towards the way the future may evolve, is not prescribed but nor can they say anything they like. As they speak into the responsiveness, verbal and non-verbal, of others present, the 'story' evolves within enabling constraints that are themselves evolving in the telling and listening. As others associate and 'fill in' an increasingly complex patterned sense-making is co-created. This is an absorbing process because a person's identity in this situation is evolving at the same time. We are not 'just talking'. We are acting together to shape ourselves and our world.

Questioner: What did flow from this meeting? Again, what changed?

Responder: Over the next few months several different activities began. The group of four at the first meeting included Walter, head of a technical section in the film manufacturing and processing business, who persuaded the manager of the European Operating Committee for the film business to move the next meeting of the EOC from Rotterdam to Ferrovia. This was an event in itself as it was considered inefficient for the committee to meet in Ferrovia because of increased travel time for many participants. He also agreed to extend the meeting for an extra day, to be hosted by people at Ferrovia. Walter and his colleagues had talked to some twenty-five other people at the plant and they were all involved in this extra day of meetings, by which they wanted to change the kind of interaction that usually occurred between members of the EOC and members of the plant. They created a new experience for all by dividing the day into five conversation spaces including lunch. Small group discussions, each lasting about an hour-and-a-half, were hosted by someone at Ferrovia in their own part of the plant. These were interspersed by returning and milling around the coffee trolleys in the main meeting room for about half-an-hour to create the next grouping that would go off to another part of the plant and talk. Being production engineers the Ferrovia people were keen to quantify their experiment and calculated that forty different conversations would have occurred and an untold number of impromptu interactions during the breaks and while wandering around the site. They accepted that some conversations would 'take off' and others not. They did not try to set an agenda of issues, trusting that such an agenda already existed. The grapevine broadcast their initiative so quite a large number of people participated along with the members of the operating committee.

Questioner: Did you continue to participate in this process?

Responder: Yes, I followed up with the people at the original meeting, encouraging them to take their own ideas seriously. I participated in the day they organized as I did in the discussions leading up to it, mostly helping to sustain the gathering confidence in taking new initiatives with unknown consequences. On the day of the big meeting I was walking between groups with the head of the business. 'Who are all these people?' he said to me. 'I've been coming to business meetings here at the plant for fifteen years and I have never met two-thirds of these people or set foot in these different parts of the plant. I had no idea how restricted my round of interaction really was.' The original difficulty with Ferrovia was the idea that it was isolated, hide-bound and difficult to penetrate. The activities I am describing began to break that particular pattern from within the interactions that were sustaining it. This is change.

Questioner: Is that it?

Responder: Not at all! Another gathering that evolved from that first meeting developed from the seeds of Alessandro's desire to discuss the way strategy for Medical Imaging was being decided. We were going over this a few weeks later when Alessandro said he felt that it would be difficult to persuade the Managing Director for Europe to join the kind of conversation he had in mind but he felt his participation would be very important. 'Why don't we try now?', I suggested, even though we had not worked out in any detail what exactly we were trying to do. So saying I picked up the phone and dialled the MD's number in Rotterdam. There was no reply from his secretary but the call was switched to the reception desk and I was told that the MD was just walking out of the door and into a taxi. Chancing my arm I asked for a very quick word. Unexpectedly I got it, the MD came to the phone and I told him that I was at Ferrovia with Alessandro who was organizing an unusual conversation to involve x and y and z and hopefully others. We wanted to open a discussion about strategy for Medical Imaging. Would he come? There was a pause and then the unambiguous response – 'I'll be there, arrange it with my secretary.' Alessandro was startled and excited by the speed of the MD's assent to a very loose proposal: 'Lets get Carlo, the head of manufacturing on board. We keep nearly having a conversation about this.' He phoned Carlo and suggested lunch. Within ten minutes we were sitting with Carlo over the Parma ham, telling him the story of the first gathering, the ideas for creating other conversations and Alessandro's own particular aspiration. As always Carlo listened carefully. Slowly his usually lugubrious features lightened – 'If we can get this to happen,' he said, 'I would take leave to be there!' It did happen. It was another rather unusual gathering taking place at Ferrovia that did not quite fit any existing group in the organization and it gave rise to further consequences.

Questioner: There seems to be a kind of serendipity at work here.

Responder: We were acting into the opportunities that were opening, conversation by conversation. The moment was ripe for this discussion and Alessandro's suggestion was seen by many as a chance to further develop their thinking together. This kind of opportunistic improvisation is always acting into the potential next steps that are almost taking shape. The art lies in moving into what might be emerging without too fixed an idea of what each move will lead to. It is not solo work, but ensemble work in which situations that are always not fully defined are further elaborated and evolved from within everyone's participation in them. It is the need to sustain relations with a diverse range of people that enables a self-organizing form of control in the movement of organizing. This process is always at work creating innovation in organizations. It is an ordinary kind of subversion where those in authority, formally accountable to sustain the status quo, must also paradoxically undermine the very order that supports their existing position for change to occur. Again this is a stance that embraces the everyday politics and ethics of change while calling for people to reflect more actively on their participation in this as a critical learning process.

Questioner: There is something appealing about what you are describing, yet I cannot believe it all runs smoothly.

Responder: No you are right. My stories continue to sound smooth because I am making a retrospective set of connections, not simple cause and effect connections but trying to illustrate self-organizing processes. In these stories I am drawing attention to the way narrative sense-making works and is at work all the time. However, if we reflect for a moment on what this process is like as we live it every day we know that it does not feel smooth at all, it is exhilarating and enjoyable and satisfying at times, but it is also frustrating, tension-filled and anxiety producing at times. Our experience of 'shaping and being shaped' is a charged emotional process in which strong feelings of inclusion and exclusion are stimulated, in which we may feel purposeful and also lost, in which our joint enterprises flourish and collapse. In later chapters, I will return to these themes.

Questioner: Your accounts are very personal, so perhaps you are describing a way of working that is unique to you?

Responder: Of course the way I work is unique to me since I am emphasizing my experience of personal participation in the processes of learning our way forward into a future of our own making. However what is not unique to me is a way of thinking about such social learning processes, a way of thinking about the processes of organizing in terms of conversational gatherings where we take action to shape and reshape the meanings of our enterprises and of ourselves. My practice reflects a process perspective that we are calling in this book series *complex responsive processes of relating.* Volume 2 of the series (Stacey 2001) develops a way of understanding how the non-linear, iterative nature of human relating, patterns itself as emergent narrative themes that organize our experience of being together, constructing identity and difference simultaneously. These themes have many aspects, including legitimate and shadow aspects. This way of thinking suggests that we are constructing together a future that is always already given shape by history but which is always open to further shaping as the simultaneous continuity and potential transformation of the patterning process of communicative action. This process is always at work in sense-making gatherings of many kinds, some long, some very short, some institutionally sponsored, others initiated in response to institutional gatherings, others involving chance events and encounters. Managers and consultants tend to pay most attention to the institutionally sponsored aspects of gathering, talking and dispersing at business meetings, away days, special workshops, carefully designed strategic conferences and so on. I have emphasized in this chapter working also with more informal processes of gathering to make sense, processes that are emerging all the time in the conduct of everyday organizational life. I want to reflect more publicly on this aspect of working and, in so doing, draw attention to and legitimize the processes of organizational continuity and change which are often rendered invisible by the dominant management discourse about how change is led or managed. This is the project of this series of books, to elaborate a thoroughly participative, less instrumental approach to organizational change, ethics and leadership.

3 The transformative activity of conversing

- Making sense from within the conduct of our conversations
- Back to Ferrovia
- Emergence at the edge of chaos
- Key themes

In Chapter 1 I referred to how difficult it is to think and talk in process terms as a participant in social sense-making or communicative action. In this chapter I will try to write as a participant sense-maker or participant-inquirer from within the movement of the social sense-making process. To further elaborate on the kind of change practice I describe in this book, I will return to Ferrovia and other episodes of the work I described in the second narrative in the last chapter (see Appendix for a list of characters introduced in these narratives). To continue to make sense of this, I find it useful to turn to what John Shotter (1993) has to say about his project to develop a *rhetorical-responsive form of social constructionism*. Shotter's interests are very close to my own. He is concerned with:

> the processes of joint action in which, and by which, people construct between themselves 'organized settings' of enabling–constraints 'into' which to direct their future actions, and how it is that sometimes those settings can become more constraining than enabling.
>
> (1993: 79)

Making sense from within the conduct of our conversations

I know there are people who find some of John Shotter's writing convoluted and strange, and indeed it can be, but then he is trying to do something rather strange and difficult. He wants to keep pointing to the open, pluralistic, changeable, incomplete, contested, negotiated nature of our communicative interaction *before*, as he sees it, we manage to impose upon it, in retrospect, a single, systematic, completed, intelligible order. This is similar to what I mean by thinking from within the movement of our participation, a movement into a paradoxical known–unknown. This social process of learning our way forward is paradoxical because the past (our personally experienced histories of social relating) help us to recognize the future and give it meaning, yet the future is also changing the meaning of the very past with which we can recognize the future. This occurs in the movement of our experience in a present that we can no longer think of as a dimensionless dot in a linear flow of time, but a present we could think of as having its own fractal time structure, in other words self-similar at all scales. In this series we have coined the term *living present* to describe such a lived-in experience of presentness, to open up for serious consideration how conversation as communicative action in the living present is transformational of personal and social realities, of the patterning of identity and difference.

Shotter does not explore the kind of paradoxical thinking that we are introducing in this series. He states that he is not setting out to develop a unified, systematic, unsituated or decontexualized theory. Rather he says he is offering us 'a tool box full of "instructive statements" or "verbal resources" for use in accounting for and making sense of our everyday conversational activities' (1993: 10). These 'tools' can serve us by drawing our attention to aspects of our experience of conversation that our more habitual ways of talking about conversation allow to go unnoticed. We can use the 'tools' to show up the indeterminate, messy nature of what goes on in ordinary conversational exchanges, and take this seriously. Like Shotter I think this is vitally necessary if we are to begin to account to ourselves for our experience of the value of free-flowing communication and the practical meaning it has for us in our actual living and organizing. I will experiment with some of Shotter's 'verbal resources' in the stories that follow which are my own 'instructive accounts'. These resources are the notions of 'developed and developing events', 'joint action', 'rational-invisibility', 'feelings of tendency', and 'the non-picturable imaginary'. These are mostly rather odd phrases that don't fall easily into existing comprehension. Thus Shotter offers them as 'tools' for shaping our sense-making experience in new ways.

Back to Ferrovia

That first gathering with Alessandro in the Medical Imaging lab, described in the last chapter, generated another strand of activity. One of the pairs who had discussed the conversations they wanted to instigate comprised a young woman, Louisa, a scientist in the research labs and a young man, Piero, in a junior management position also in the labs. When Doug and I were back in Ferrovia some weeks after that first meeting we discovered that Piero was very reluctant to take another step. He seemed dogged by fears of a heavy hand on his shoulder suggesting that it would be in his interest to lie low and not stir things up. Not that this had happened, but he felt it might. Louisa, on the contrary, believed that stirring things up a bit would be very helpful. She introduced us to Lorenzo, another research scientist, who shared her restlessness under what they experienced as a rather strict regime in the labs. They had been talking to a number of their colleagues and wanted us to meet with a group of them. Doug and I suggested that we would come over to the labs. It was surprising to feel their wariness about gathering in the labs themselves. They suggested we meet them right after lunch in the room on the ground floor of the guest house where we were staying, across the road from the plant. Perhaps gathering and talking has always been experienced as a potentially subversive activity: 'just' talking, we are aware, may disturb the status quo.

When we arrived at the guest house we found more than twenty people seated round a large table in a shuttered room, so that the lights were needed in the bright sun of an Italian afternoon. There was a loud hum of conversation. As ever the level of English comprehension amongst the Italians was reasonably good, but confidence in speaking it much less. For Doug and myself, this was even more true of our Italian. There was a vibrant air of energy and expectancy as our conversation began.

Let us pause here a moment and use one of Shotter's tools, that of paying attention to conversational situations as *developed and developing events*. In the situation above quite a large number of people had gathered to talk, but it is not easy to say what about. What was the topic of conversation? As Shotter points out, in the course of our participation in conversation 'what is being talked about' is at many points necessarily unclear as we take and afford each other opportunities to come to know what we are talking about from within the development of the conversation itself. This is true even when a topic has supposedly been set or agreed in advance. And, as the conversation develops, it is not a question of one person saying something and others listening to 'understand' and then formulate a response in a tidy manner. Rather, conversation has peculiar spatial and temporal properties, which I have referred to already as the qualities of the *living present*. In oral encounters of reciprocal speech something very different is going on than the orderly way we tend to later represent it, especially in written form. In oral encounters we speak into one another's responses, not in a simple 'first one, then the next', kind of way. Rather, we find ourselves responsively shaping our utterances to one another in the very process of speaking and listening. We are responding to the particular circumstances of each utterance even as we are contributing to the development of those circumstances. We find ourselves saying what we did not realize we 'thought'. What is said later is serving all the time to develop what was meant earlier and this looping back and forth between people in space and time means that we are always on the way to shaping something never fully achieved. We are 'reforming' and 'transforming' in a very practical way the movement of our possible stances and actions in relation to one another and other aspects of our circumstances in order to 'make possible' how and where to go on from here. It is a 'here' that we are busily fashioning from the resources of the 'past' made afresh in this 'living present' that is becoming significant in new ways in the light of future channels of possible action we are thus opening up.

This is a radically different way of noticing what is going on in the actual experience of conversation compared to our usual preoccupation with what we insist we are doing – clarifying information, reaching shared understandings, developing orderly agreements and plans and capturing outputs. These usual pre-occupations have, to use another of Shotter's tools, made very important aspects of our experience of conversation *rationally-invisible* to us. We cannot notice much of what we are actually doing together because it has no place in the dominant discourse that purports to describe what we are doing!

I once had the experience of watching a video of a conversation in which I had participated a day or two earlier. The conversation was recorded by chance. All ten of us involved had spoken subsequently of our experience of this as a taut, tension filled, highly charged, difficult and productive negotiation. It arose amongst a group of us responsible for conducting a large conference sponsored by the government and other agencies in Malaysia. The start of the conference was imminent and there was serious disagreement in the group. We had gathered to talk through our differences. We had all been keyed up, concentrating hard, following every gesture and word, utterly absorbed in the communicative process unfolding between us all. To our astonishment when several of us later watched the video, the drama we all remembered was absent. The scene we watched was rather hard to concentrate on, almost boring, and the development of the conversation hard to follow. The emotional qualities seemed much less intense than any of us had experienced. Observing ourselves converse, from outside the experience, as it were, even we could not grasp the significance of what was going on in the same way we could when we were engaged in that conversation as a living experience. Far from thinking that watching the video gave us a more accurate 'overview' of what had happened, we found it almost laughable, a severely diminished record. What we 'knew' of that conversation could only be known from within the conduct of it, yet the knowledge we generated together in the course of it was very practical. We organized ourselves to be able to carry on working in productive and innovative ways together despite not having reached any really 'shared' understandings that we could later point to.

This is the paradoxical nature of what I believe Shotter (1984) means by *joint action* which he points out always produces unintended and unpredictable outcomes. People generate between themselves, 'without conscious realisation of the fact, a changing sea of moral enablements and constraints, of privileges and entitlements, and obligations and sanctions – in short, an ethos' (1993: 39). Such evolving 'organised practical-moral settings' cannot be traced back to the intentions of any one of us and so it is *as if* this setting or situation that we co-create has, for us, a 'given' or 'externally caused' nature. However as we are tempted to literalize or reify such a setting in terms of an image or model, we falsely complete what is essentially always vague and open to further shaping. The organization of the setting continues to emerge in a self-organizing way as people interweave their communicative action and that organization continues to invite and motivate and limit our next possible actions as we continue to communicate.

Let us return to the room in Ferrovia with the sun piercing the slats of the shutters and the diverse group of research scientists gathered together. We embark once again on a messy conversation of multiple threads, themes and fragments. We begin somehow with the searching backwards to make some sense of coming together. The conversation runs along the following narrative themes, mostly exploring issues of inclusion–exclusion and mutually held constraints–enablements: that first meeting with Allesandro and the others. How come Louisa was invited? What had prevented others from coming? What had happened since then? The accounts various people had heard of the initiative taken by their colleagues in the film business of which I have already written in the last chapter. How a number of people would have liked to have joined those conversations with members of the film operating committee. How they understood the process of who was invited. What had prevented them from taking the initiative themselves to join in. Memories of meeting me by chance on a visit to the labs some months ago. The suggestion I had made that it might be valuable to create some informal forums of exchange across different parts of the site. Their reluctance to do this without checking the approval of the head of the labs. Their feeling that I had not understood why they felt so constrained. The frustration they had felt with the organized brainstorming sessions in the plant. The official open-door policy of management. The narrow kind of dialogue possible between managers and staff in the labs themselves. How it was always possible to go to speak with any manager, but it was not possible to *explore* issues with them. If you were clear about what you wanted to know or what you wanted to suggest, no problem, but there was no discussion. Of course they spoke among themselves and no doubt managers spoke informally between themselves but points of contact for freer flowing exchange between the layers were sparse indeed. But the spin-off meant a smaller organization, less formality, more open exchange. Why were they waiting for the managers to start this, what stopped them taking the initiative? I said something like: 'I have no doubt that Carlo [head of manufacturing and one of the most senior managers at the site, already referred to in Chapter 2] would be delighted to have some of you knocking on his door and suggesting lunch.' This idea caused pandemonium in the room. Many people were talking at once, arguing, agreeing and disagreeing. Some were all for phoning Carlo immediately, others shouting them down, others suggesting that the best place to start would be their own managers in the lab. Quietly Doug and I said that we would be very happy to support them and talk more with them, but for now we needed to go. As we passed the gates to the plant we paused to telephone Carlo. 'What would be your reaction,' I asked, 'if you got a group of young people from the labs asking you to lunch?' 'When is this dream going to happen?' laughed Carlo, 'I only wish they would.' 'Well, you might be surprised,' I said.

During the afternoon we managed to find an occasion to fall in with Eduardo, the head of the research labs, as we took the long walk between the Dirigenti building and the labs. This gave us some insights. He was probably the most deeply introverted man I have ever encountered. To sustain conversation with him that was not on a very clear-cut issue or on a crisp question and answer basis was a near impossible struggle. Very quickly a reciprocal awkwardness arose that made parting a relief. The space for mutual anxiety to develop was great. We also had a chat with Roberto, the other senior manager of the labs. We discovered that what Eduardo epitomized in reclusiveness, Roberto matched in geniality and reassurance, so that attempts at real exploration were overwhelmed with a convivial rendering of all issues as over-rated, unimportant, recently solved, or about to be solved. The labs were held in an effective vice between these two in which new conversations about what was going on had difficulty getting started.

Over the next few months we learned that the lab staff initiated a series of luncheons. Each of the managers on the Site Committee were asked to join a group of laboratory staff for lunch. Each time the invitation was made in person and different groups of people were involved. The point of the lunches was to talk together about what was happening in the company from everyone's different perspectives. We heard from Louisa that even Eduardo had surprised everyone by relaxing a little in this new setting, becoming more open, friendly and forthcoming. This initiative was highly valued by all concerned.

Let us pause again here. People in conversation are shaping and shifting the web of enabling–constraints in which they are enmeshed. They are constructing their future not as a single 'vision' or a set of goals, but in terms of what courses of action become possible and sensible for them in their evolving circumstances as they communicate. Again I think one of Shotter's tools is useful here. I have often talked of the way a group of people work with tantalizing 'glimpses' of partially formed sense-making, glimpsed in different ways by different people. This visual imagery currently dominates our metaphors of sense-making, so that we are always talking of seeing things this way or that, taking a view, shifting perspective and so on. This metaphor sustains our perception of ourselves cognitively manipulating 'objects' of thought as products of our talk. Shotter suggests that we could notice the *feelings of tendency* that we are shaping in our speaking together, a phrase he takes from the writings of William James (1890). This is helpful in reminding us that conversation is not a purely intellectual activity. When we converse we are not decoding words and sentences as signs which represent some object to which we are referring, nor are we simply interpreting bodily signals from others as a 'mental' activity. Rather we are immersed in a sensuous flow of patterned feeling, a kind of ethos in which words 'in their speaking' have the power to 'move' or 'arrest' us, shift our perceptions and actions because we are communicating as intelligent bodies. The situations we construct together involve incomplete, developing tendencies arising from a social history of enabling–constraints. These tendencies cannot be wholly grasped in mental representations, rather as we converse we 'give form to feeling', so that what at first is a mere felt tendency can be eventually realized as a new form of organization and eventually social institution. It is this process that Doug and I were involved in with the people from the labs as they came to feel able to undertake action that had recently felt frustratingly 'impossible'. The patterns of mutual constraint–enablement shifted from within the processes of communication which were sustaining them. This is again a very different understanding from currently fashionable notions of empowerment.

Let us wind back further in time at Ferrovia to the way the possibilities of our involvement there began. I want to illustrate how change occurs in the move from conversation to conversation, connection to connection, association to association in which the 'terrain' of action is being constructed or, as Shotter puts it, we interweave our actions in order to go on together. I also want to indicate how this differs from the way the activities of consulting are usually framed in terms of a rational cyclical process of intial contacts and contracting, data gathering and analysis–synthesis, feedback, joint diagnosis, action, implementation, review and disengagement.

As the talk of concern about Ferrovia swirled about in various conversations in other parts of the company during the early part of this assignment, my colleague Doug and I decided it would be useful to make a visit there. We decided to contact the one member of the site committee at Ferrovia that we had already met. This was Carlo, the head of manufacturing, whose name has cropped up already several times. He had attended a small seminar that Doug and I had led before the spin-off. We had discussed the implications of 'complexity' ideas and a sympathetic rapport with Carlo had been established.

Doug spoke to him on the phone and explained the background of our interest in the plant and our hope to visit him and his colleagues at Ferrovia. We wanted to talk about their experience of the significance of the changes taking place and what impact this was having at the plant. He was immediately responsive and said he would organize a get together of the management team.

Why go through Carlo? We could easily have set up this meeting with the Site Manager as part of our official engagement with the company.

However, speaking with Carlo drew on the history of our previous conversations. This enabled us to agree a next practical action with very little of the usual rational justifications about goals and outcomes of the trip. We were taking exploratory action whose meaning we would come to know.

So in May, before the legal separation of the spin-off company, Doug and I flew to Italy, rented a car and took the swooping road through the hills to the plant, nestling in its valley, nearly three hours' drive away.

We inquired at the gate-house and were escorted to the Dirigenti building to see Carlo. He greeted us warmly and led us immediately to a rather sombre panelled conference room where ten Italian dark-suited managers were already gathered. The room was set up for presentations as such rooms in organizations so often are, but we said we simply wanted to sit and talk with them. There was some surprise but also pleasure; they were accustomed to people coming to talk to or at them, at least in the setting of the conference room. We told again how we came to be involved with the company at this time, of our previous connection with Carlo and our interest in what was happening at the plant since its name seemed to be on many people's lips. What sense were they making of the new situation and other people's concerns?

The conversation meandered something like this: here change was not real to people – the strength of the place was its continuity. 'This is not a place of careers, people are born and die here.' 'It's like Japan – work for life.' To the employees this latest change was just a change of nameplate and even then only the big nameplates; little signs on the bicycles, the drink mats, the door mats, the notice-boards – these still bore the name of the old company. In other parts of Europe, the spin-off had produced great stress, redundancies, changes in jobs, but here what had changed really? We're all doing the same work as before, the same pressures as before, just a flurry of visitors, news bulletins, exhortations to create a very different culture. It was clear that Doug and I could easily be just part of this 'flurry'.

Roberto, head of the research lab came in:

> There is concern at the centre that we're weighed down with
> complication, bureaucracy, waste of money, too top heavy,
> unnecessary jobs. But we are already dealing with this. We're proud
> that we have managed carefully a small slimming down at the spin-off
> with minimum disruption to people's sense of security. Of course

we're all sitting here, the same managers, the same conversation . . .
The existing culture permeates everything. Perhaps we're not
conscious of how heavy the presence of that culture is.

It transpired that he and one of the other managers, Fulvio, were leading
a small task force consisting of a few members of the site committee on
Communications – how to work out a plan for informing people of the
impact of the spin-off. How would this help, we asked, if, as they had
been saying, people *experienced* nothing as different? Surely this would
make the talk of change seem even more unreal. Could we maybe join
this task force and participate in the discussions? There was polite assent
but I felt that we had hit the guarded fence that kept outsiders from the
plant's own conversations. 'Of course,' said Roberto, 'but you know
many people's English is not that good . . . it is inhibiting to free
discussion.'

Franco, the youngest man on the team, insisted that there were stirrings
of change. 'We have been screened from the businesses in the past, now
we are developing a more external focus, contacting customers directly,
bringing them into the plant.'

Carlo sighed:

But I fear this is just another programme. We are handed one
programme after another, like medicines. 'Champions', 'Growing
Together', now 'Customer First'. They are superficial. But now
maybe things could be different. Whatever you say about us dealing
with slimming down, Roberto, there will be cuts, cuts, paring down,
decisions all made at the top. But then the plant itself will find out
how to make all this actually work. This is the real source of change.
It is no good insisting on straight lines through problems.

I listened with interest. This was the voice I remembered from the
seminar. Carlo had an intuitive feel for the nature of self-organization,
but it had given him a world-weary sadness about the futility of
managerial attempts at control. Doug began talking about the concept of
emergence as a way of understanding what Carlo was saying. One of the
other managers, Cesare, who had been silent until now, shrugged in
agreement. Of course you could never design a real working company –
it developed itself. The formal structure is not the organization. 'IT, HR –
these functions become baronies trying to flood the organization with
policies, but they are staffed with people who remain inattentive to, or
afraid to talk about, what is really happening.' I was struck by this
instinct among some of the Italians for the paradoxical tension between

the legitimate institutions of the company and its apparently rule-governed patterns and the shadowy nature of everyday organizing whose nature was always open and evolving. I said that maybe the plant could be the seedbed of another way of understanding how complex change emerges. There was an astonished pause. Then Roberto smiled broadly. 'This is the first time in my memory,' he said, 'that anyone has come to this plant and suggested that we Italians might have something valuable to offer. Maybe there is a wind of change after all!' This felt far from a straightforward remark.

We said we would like to find ways to work in the plant in the spirit of the email message that we had already arranged to be sent out throughout the company via the internal email system. In this note we had suggested that we would like to join the ongoing conversations in the company about the meaning of what was happening. There were promises to contact us. We were taken to lunch in the dining room and offered a tour of the factory, then a car was ordered to take us to the seaside hotel where reservations had been made for us. There were no local hotels near the factory we were told. We began to understand how difficult it could be to penetrate the life of the plant.

We are not interviewing or gathering data here. We are not trying to piece together a picture of a set of issues and relationships at the plant or between the plant and other parts of the company. We sat in the bar at the hotel and talked, sharing impressions covering all sorts of memories, stories, speculations and ideas. We came to a decision that it would be interesting to visit the Milan office where the parent company was based and learn more about how people made sense of Ferrovia's history and its new role. We were engaged in prospective rather than retrospective sense-making – how to make sense of a next step in an improvised, incomplete narrative. This is very different from trying to model or picture our understanding of a situation. Our 'task' was to help change the 'culture' and like our talk of 'society' or 'self' these are ideas which Shotter calls the *not picturable imaginary*.

Shotter suggests that such concepts are imaginary forms, always ambiguous and not fully developed and we try to capture their tendencies of feeling at our peril. He warns that when we are tempted to 'complete' such ideas, by modelling or picturing them, we move to formulating them as 'imagined' or 'imaginable' entities. Then we risk creating an enclosed and mechanical form of social life in which we risk trapping ourselves. This is what happens when we try to describe cultures as picturable systems. Such pictures are spatially complete entities with all their parts and relationships simultaneously present. Doing this distracts attention from the process of *prospective sense-making*, by which we creatively respond to each other *over time* to shape our practical knowledge of how to go on in ways that we can account to one another for. And the point is that these ways of accounting for ourselves and our actions are evolving as we communicate. That is how our organizing changes over time, which is not to be confused with developing policies and blueprints for redesigning institutions as conceptual entities which are picturable.

The next day we called the HR manager in Milan, who we knew from previous work in the 'parent' company, and asked if we could drop by on our way to the airport as we had spent the previous day at Ferrovia. He said that he would see if Maurizio, the head of the Italian Region might also be free. The four of us met in the afternoon in the Milan headquarters. We said a little about our visit to Ferrovia. I said that I thought there was considerable potential at the plant to be worked with. Maurizio scoffed openly. Did I not understand? This was an emergency! Change was needed fast and the plant would never change. 'However,' he said with grim satisfaction, 'we have delivered one shock, we have appointed someone from Naples to improve the manufacturing quality. They won't like having a Southern Italian amongst the old guard.' I remembered the relatively quiet Cesare. I suggested that Maurizio's persistence in seeing the plant in this closed way would hardly contribute to helping it change. Maurizio became heated. I did not understand. The plant was a lost cause. It was only a matter of time before its activities would be transferred to the US. I was unmoved by this. Who knows what would happen? People all over the spin-off company were talking with interest and concern about the plant. Doug and I would explore what work we might do there. Maurizio raised his eyebrows. Did we have the agreement of Giorgio, the senior manager at the plant? I said we had not met him yet, as he had been travelling yesterday, but we had met and talked with the other members of the site committee. We were not intending to run a formal programme, but to involve ourselves with people in whatever way we could find. Maurizio's eyebrows shot up higher. I felt that he found me irritating, he could not quite place the power relations that made sense of the way I was talking. Alberto, the HR manager, who had sat silent throughout this meeting, said later that he thought this was a good exchange. Maurizio had apparently said he had no more than five minutes to spare to meet with us, but the conversation had lasted well over an hour. 'I think he was unsettled,' smiled Alberto. 'It's good. No one ever challenges him.' 'If you agreed with some of what I said, could you not have voiced this?' I asked him. 'Oh, you know,' he shrugged, 'there's no point.'

Doug and I did not try to make any summary of these visits to feedback to anyone anywhere. As we continued to meet and talk with people in other settings we would bring up some memory of our encounters and compare experiences with others. For example, this kind of conversation led to the napkin list that later led me to call Alessandro as I have already described in Chapter 2. But this was some months away.

Only two weeks after this first visit to Ferrovia, I received a phone call from Cesare. 'You said it was possible to invite you to join some of our discussions. I feel I need help. I am trying to work with a team of people from all over the plant to improve manufacturing quality, but I am coming up against a kind of wall. Will you come to our next meeting?'

I wondered how to make more of another trip to Italy. I phoned Roberto and Fulvio who had talked about the communications task force and asked if they might be convening another meeting soon. They prevaricated but said that they would be delighted to talk more with me whenever I came again. At that point I knew no one else at the plant. A few days later I received a fax from a Gianni, in the Processing Chemistry R&D laboratory at Ferrovia. A few days before he had received the public email message that had been sent out from Doug and myself. His fax was written in convoluted English, apologizing about the lack of clarity. It made an analogy between the plant and a car, which I had difficulty grasping, but the main point seemed to be that no matter what kind of car it was, only if it was moving did it have any success because then intuitions and serendipity were involved. Intrigued, I called him. He was delighted when I told him that he was the only person in the plant who had accepted the invitation to respond to our message. This seemed to confirm something for him. 'People do nothing. We wait to avoid mistakes. We must move the car and learn from mistakes, try only to avoid head-on crashes when you are moving through a new unexplored way.' He insisted on faxing twenty pages of an English book he was reading about the impact of chance events in history – serendipity. I said I was shortly coming to Ferrovia, could we meet? Could he introduce me to other colleagues interested to talk about what was happening? Yes, Yes. I would find him in the lab.

This time I made the long drive to Ferrovia alone. My muscles were tense from gripping the wheel as I drove in and out of the dazzling brightness and sudden darkness of the tunnels through the mountains. I was too nervous to fully appreciate the extraordinary beauty of the scenery and the road itself, a feat of aesthetic daring typical of Italian engineers. I met Cesare in his office in the Dirigenti building. He was obviously relieved to talk:

> I think this is the end of my career. I came here because I had been successful in improving the quality at another plant that has now closed in the reorganization. I was welcomed here and I gave a presentation to the site committee about what I wanted to do. They seemed willing to help. They suggested a team of people to work with me who are already engaged in different kinds of quality projects in different parts of the plant. It is a mess; there are many different people in isolated compartments concerned with quality as it affects them. They refuse to be interested in the impact of different quality requirements in another area. No one is willing to talk directly with counterparts in other parts of the plant. Everything is referred to a superior and nothing happens. I have good meetings with this group, we draw up plans for collecting data, suggesting improvements, but as soon as some real experiment is needed, suddenly it is not the right time, there are no resources to implement anything. We try to collect useful data and it is a farce, nothing is consistent from one area to another, no one is willing to make changes. I question some strange figures and I'm told, 'Oh yes that's so and so, he is always measuring incorrectly so we just automatically adjust his figures upwards.'

All the time he was talking, Cesare sketched diagrams, pulling across one sheet of paper after another, memos he has written, reports by the group. He was agitated, confused by his sense of failure in a situation he didn't fully understand. Something subtle, he felt, was opposing his endeavours. Had he talked with anyone about his concerns and frustrations? No. I sensed he may not have wanted to admit that things were not working – he carried the pleasure of a previous success and was reluctant to accept publicly that it was not going to be so easy here. I remembered the gleeful look on Maurizio's face when he spoke of Cesare's appointment. I wondered how much he was expected to fail, to demonstrate the impossibility of change at Ferrovia.

Tentatively I mentioned that I knew he was from Naples and had been told there may be some unspoken resentment at his appointment among other members of the site committee. Yes, he had felt this. He kept himself to himself. He had left his family behind and was staying at the guest lodge over the road during the week. I pricked up my ears. What guest lodge? The buildings across the way are owned by the company and can be used for overnight or longer stays. Could I stay there? Yes, of course. They are not much used. Everyone stays at the coast. No one even suggested it as an option, I said, even though it takes over an hour to drive to the coast. I began to realize this was one of many ways we all sustained the habitual experience of Ferrovia keeping its visitors at bay. Cesare agreed to organize a room for me and to cancel my hotel booking.

I did not discuss with Cesare what role he wanted me to take at the meeting. Instead my involvement was based on the idea that I would 'join' the meeting which leaves unspecified in advance of interacting what the 'rules' of interaction should be. Far from ignoring the potential of the difference created by my presence, this leaves room for us to explore what significance we will all make of this together. Again I do not mean simply that this becomes an early item to be sorted out at the start of the meeting but as an ongoing part of working together. In this respect I am drawing attention to how identities are always at play for all of us. As I showed in the last chapter, a recurring theme of organizing is the question 'Who are we and what are we all doing here?' It is a question we are repeatedly asking and responding to so that the identity of groups and individuals is simultaneously sustained and changed.

People were beginning to gather in the corridor for Cesare's meeting so we moved out of the office to greet them. They were a whole generation younger than the people I had met so far, both men and women. We trooped back into the conference room I knew from before. Cesare introduced me. 'This is Patricia. She helps with our company becoming something new. I asked her to come and talk with us. She spoke to the site committee already. It was very interesting.' They all looked at me expectantly. I suggested that we abandon the primary use of English. 'My Italian is minimal. I will speak in English, but please feel free to speak together in Italian. I will ask for translation when I need it. Cesare has been talking with me just now about some of the difficulties he is experiencing.' There followed an exhausting but exhilarating couple of hours. Cesare launched into an only slightly constrained version of what he had been saying to me earlier. It was as though talking to me, and in some way my presence, loosened any reservations he had felt about opening up this conversation. He was rapidly interrupted in Italian and responded in his native tongue. I quickly lost the detail but I could sense the surprise, agreement and anger around the table. I guessed possible content from the flow of emotions, gesticulations, expressions as chairs were pulled back, people stood up and walked around. I began to join in, asking questions, making comments.

Several members of the group shared Cesare's frustrations. They had begun to enjoy this work together taking a broader view of the overall quality in the plant. They liked the ideas that Cesare had brought, but crossing departments in the plant was unprecedented. Many of them felt in tension between their fledgling sense of involvement in this group and their loyalty to their bosses, who wanted them to put the interests of a particular area first. Some felt under considerable pressure to withdraw from the group. I asked about what was familiar about how they were approaching this project. Were there any ways they could be more experimental in how they worked, rather than seeing experiments only in terms of quality improvements? The conversation flowed out of the conference room and downstairs to the espresso machine, where we all stood around for a good 45 minutes instead of returning.

A member of the group asked Cesare about how he was communicating with his colleagues on the site committee. He said he gave regular progress reports by a formal presentation at meetings. Otherwise, he admitted, he was a bit of a loner. I asked what was stopping them asking one or two of the managers to join their meetings? This was unprecedented. I encouraged them to think how they would be able to talk very differently with one or two of the more sympathetic managers about what they were trying to do and some of the obstacles they were encountering. Enlist their understanding and support, perhaps manage to shift the dialogue that went on between their bosses about this project. It also became clear that the remit to improve quality came from the European management team of the company. Cesare's appointment had been strongly backed by Donald, the Operations MD. I asked what would happen if they invited Donald to come to talk with this team about the changes going on and the new challenges facing the company. 'But,' said Cesare, 'when he visits the plant, he has a full set of meetings prearranged.' 'Why not become one of those arrangements? You know him a little, Cesare. Call him. Tell him you need him to come and help set this project in the wider context of what is going on.' The eyes of the young people sparkled – I felt they were hungry for more direct engagement with the world beyond Ferrovia. They were accustomed to management briefings cascading down the line or official presentations by visiting senior management.

As small groupings formed around the coffee machine and I drank yet another viciously strong shot of caffeine, one of the young men, Piero, drew me aside. His eyes were worried, his face sombre. It was very difficult for him being involved in this project, he felt that it went against his boss's preferences for keeping issues within the department. He felt he was being disloyal, revealing the undoubted problems that there were. It would not be good for his prospects at the plant if his boss no longer trusted him. I asked whether he believed his boss knew that there were problems with quality that could be overcome. He said that he had once tried to defend a report that the quality group had produced which criticized aspects of the procedures in his boss's department and his boss had been angry and dismissive, saying that Cesare did not understand the intricacies and difficulties of the film coating process and his methods would do more harm than good. Another member of the team, overhearing some of this, joined us, to agree that this particular manager was very difficult. I beckoned Cesare over and asked him if he realized how members of his team were experiencing the pressures of working on this project. Emboldened, the young man spoke in Italian to Cesare, who turned and said that the trouble was that it was impossible to open up any discussion of this in the site committee. Everyone there had worked together for years and somehow closed ranks. The manager under discussion was known to be very authoritarian but he was responsible for creating the original coating process used in the plant, his knowledge was very valuable and he ran the plant well. No one wanted to disturb the situation. I sensed that no one really tried – the prohibitions that were jointly sustained around all this were so strongly felt by everyone that the pattern had great stability. The meeting ended.

We did not attempt to make any summary or agree any action plans. I said to Cesare that I thought it would be useful to see what flowed from the conversation of that morning. Cesare was pleased. He felt that the group had broken through a self-created limit on what could be discussed and the whole feeling of the discussion had been very different. He seemed excited.

We passed Carlo in the corridor as we left the conference room and fell into step with him. I suggested that perhaps we could all three go to lunch? 'Yes, good,' said Carlo. We chatted over the antipasta. Carlo ordered some wine. I asked about staying in the guest house. Carlo said that would be no problem. Most people preferred to have access to the restaurants and facilities of the coastal town. I said I would rather be free to come and go at the plant. After a while, I said that we had had a lively meeting with the Quality group that morning. 'I expect you realize, Carlo,' I said, 'what a difficult job Cesare and his people are having trying to work across the customary boundaries.' Carlo looked down at the checked cloth and then met my gaze. 'Yes,' he sighed, 'attitudes are slow to change ...' 'Look,' I said, 'it's no good the members of the site committee talking to me about how they are leading change, setting up communication task forces – what matters is how a real project like this is handled.' Carlo turned to Cesare, 'Maybe we should talk ...' Cesare seized the moment – 'We spoke this morning about asking you to join our next meeting so that we can talk about what we are trying to do, how the difficulties arise.' 'OK,' said Carlo, 'I'll bring Roberto also. He understands the problems. Maybe we can find ways ...'

Had I formulated in advance an intention to talk to Carlo after Cesare's meeting? Did I have an objective in mind as I suggested lunch? The answer to both questions is 'no, not exactly, yes in part perhaps, but it is not quite like that'! That is not to say that I am acting randomly or without intention. Intentions are forming all the time, not as fully completed plans of campaign but as movements into the way things seem to be shaping up. Intentions, mine and others, are forming and evolving responsively. I am 'feeling my way forward' in a web of shifting circumstances that I am participating in creating – as I suggest we all do all the time.

I excused myself at this point, saying that I had made an appointment to see some people in the Chemistry Lab. This was the connection I had made with Gianni, he of the interests in serendipity. Carlo looked startled. Did I need an escort? No, no, I said. No escort. I would find my way. I would ask people.

As I walked around the buildings with their huge pipes and chimneys, over a bridge and round to the research labs, I felt that I had begun to slip past the fine gauze of habitual interaction that kept visitors to the restricted path between gatehouse, Dirigenti building and management dining room. After asking a number of people, I found my way to the office of Gianni, who was waiting for me with a couple of colleagues. I began again a conversation about the kind of work that Doug and I were trying to do and asked them about their experiences. Had the spin-off made much difference to them? Not as yet. There had been an open day on 1st June to celebrate the change of name and there had been picnics in the grounds with employees' families and some speeches and posters. They worked for Eduardo, the manager who had been described as difficult that morning. They said that some big meetings were being organized the following week to discuss the impact of the changes in the labs. They showed me a memo about it. I couldn't understand the Italian but could see a timetable that seemed to consist of three half-hour talks by different managers and 20 minutes for questions and answers at the end. There had also been some brainstorming sessions in which people had been asked for ideas about improvements at the plant.

I asked if any of the three of them were hoping that the spin-off would bring some needed changes. They wanted to be more directly connected to the businesses, to customers. Their research work kept them isolated from this. All discussions about the shift towards digital processing and computer imaging products that were seen as part of the firm's future seemed to occur far away from them. They had been reassured that there was still a future in chemical processing – the markets of Eastern Europe, for example, and specialist photography, but they were restless, clearly having their own sources of information in general terms about the photo-chemical industry and its predicted demise. Did they not have their own links and contacts with friends and colleagues in other parts of the company or, indeed, at the plant in which information was shared and discussed? Not so much, not as much as they would like. Would it be useful to create a forum of some kind at the plant to pool knowledge and develop responses? They liked this idea but when I said this would be easy to just start informally with their existing contacts and let it expand, they were uneasy. They would need to discuss such an initiative with Eduardo. Why could we just not do it? They seemed puzzled – to them it was obvious why not. OK, I said, think about it. Talk with some colleagues. Raise this with Eduardo. They said they would, but I doubted it somehow.

Did I expect to be able to say what the result or impact of such a conversation might be? No, not at all. I was creating history (with a small 'h') whose meaning might turn out to become significant some time later. This attitude, that says I cannot know the meaning of my activities before acting, invites me to be as present as possible to the improvisational possibilities of what I am doing.

I left and walked back to the gatehouse. I was tired, but I had arranged to meet with Roberto and Fulvio. Back to the Dirigenti building, where the two managers were already together, eager to show me the plans of the meetings they were organizing. I said I had seen the timetable already and wondered if it was not possible to allow more time for a freer flow of discussion amongst those gathered, rather than giving them three speeches. We have already had a brainstorming session, they said. What did that produce, I asked? Oh, nothing very substantial, a few ideas about the use of telephones and a reorganization of the offices. I talked about other ways in which large meetings might be handled. Roberto was interested but said it was too late to alter the arrangements now. I suggested that I could join these sessions, but they did not think it was worth my coming back so soon. They would let me know how the meetings went. I knew I was being warmly brushed off.

As I left, I saw the door of the site manager's office open and, looking in, I presumed it must be Giorgio, the site manager, sitting at his desk. I knocked and entered and introduced myself. He was a gentle-faced man with a mild manner. He looked very tired. He apologized for missing the meeting when Doug and I had talked with the site committee. I sat down and told him about my day and my impressions. He said that he felt this was a calm before the storm, that no one realized what new demands were going to be made and how very different the pressures would be. I said that I felt that the networks of conversation in the plant were caught in some repetitive eddies. Doug and I would like to try to stir up some much wider conversations within the plant and link these to others in the rest of the company. We needed to be able to come and go freely, get to know people, create some informal forums and meetings, ask questions, encourage people to make connections and take initiatives without going through the usual channels of permission and approval. 'I wanted you to know that this is what Doug and I will be doing without knowing where all this will lead.' He looked at me gravely. 'We need this,' he said. 'It will not be easy. The managers, we are all used to the old ways, we do not really know how to stimulate change.' I said, 'I think you are reaping all the existing prejudices about this place. People are pessimistic about the capacity for change here and will be quick to blame Ferrovia for belonging to the past. I have a sense already of how some limits are being sustained. I won't keep coming to check with you, but please contact me if you want to talk with me.' He said that he already had some sense of what my involvement at the plant might mean. Carlo had come to talk with him that afternoon about Cesare's Quality Team and the need to give stronger backing to an approach to quality that crossed the usual divisions.

I went to the gate to pick up the key to the guest house. The rooms were spacious and comfortable, infinitely preferable in my view to the plastic modernity of the coastal hotel. I lay back on the bed and fell immediately asleep, exhausted by the day's dense impressions.

In early August I was again in Italy with a joint meeting of all the HR managers from the US and Europe. I called Cesare who suggested driving over from the plant to tell me how things were going. He was in a much more buoyant mood. Carlo and Roberto had joined the team's next meeting and there had been, he felt, a remarkably frank discussion. He felt that he had new allies and was less isolated. There had been some changes to membership of his team, some people had withdrawn suggesting replacements and others had been invited. Some real experimentation was now underway in several areas. There was a lot still to do, but he no longer felt his task was impossible. When Donald, the European MD, had made a visit to the plant in July, Cesare had suggested meeting for breakfast and Donald later made a point of asking for a progress report from him at the meeting with the rest of the site committee. He had asked detailed questions, emphasized how important it was for the project to produce results fast. He had asked several managers around the table for their views of progress with the initiative in their area. Cesare was delighted. The coded message in the formal setting was crystal clear. He asked if I could join his group again later in the autumn. He felt the conversation the last time, messy though it had been, had shifted the group's self-perception. Instead of seeing themselves as co-opted onto a dicey project, they now considered themselves pioneers, vanguards of change at the plant. I agreed.

It was a few weeks' later that I called Alessandro with my napkin list and the story I told in the last chapter evolved.

What am I drawing attention to throughout this practice narrative? Precisely those aspects of how things change that is usually missing from orderly accounts of organization change initiatives. The random as well as intended encounters, the opportunism, the making connections purposefully but without a set of clearly defined objectives, the participating fully in situations of which I had only a very incomplete grasp, of moving in the flow of events and so affecting them in unknowable ways. This account is instructive of continuity and change as *emergence* in the complex social processes of communicative action. Let us look at how this concept of emergence has come to be linked with that of self-organization and the metaphor of 'the edge of chaos' in the natural sciences.

Emergence at the edge of chaos

The intriguing image of the edge of chaos was first introduced among scientists at the Santa Fe Institute in New Mexico who were exploring the behaviour of computer simulated complex networks of digital symbols or 'agents'. Each digital agent in such a simulation is a set of interaction rules, expressed as computer instructions, interacting locally with other agents, in the absence of any global instruction set. In other words, in such networks it is not that every agent is connected to every other at the same time, but that each is connected to a variable number of 'neighbours' and so there is the potential for connectivity across the network over time. There is no programme for the network overall, except the initial settings created by the investigating programmer. In some cases each agent can only follow a single set of interacting rules, sometimes the agents can 'learn' or evolve their instruction sets as a result of interacting. The complexity is created by the fact that all the agents are responding to one another's signals all the time in an iterative, non-linear dynamic. Kauffman (1995) explored in particular the behaviour of Boolean nets, which are networks of large numbers of binary elements with simple on/off switching rules. Langton (1992) explored cellular automata, whose elements are capable of more than two values, while Ray (1992) also explored genetic algorithms. What the scientists were simulating were various kinds of networks of interaction as 'systems' identified and studied in nature – interacting genes in the genome, interacting neurons in the brain, interacting ants in a colony, flocking birds and so on. The question was: how did organization, or pattern, emerge in such networks, how did they self-organize?

These scientists showed that simulations of the interaction of very large numbers of such digital 'agents' always exhibited three broad regimes of patterning behaviour. This depends on the number and strength of connections between agents, the diversity of agents and the intensity of information flows between them, or, in other words, the intensity of interaction due to the mutual sensitivity or responsiveness of the agents. In some conditions (low connectivity, low diversity, sluggish interaction) the simulations develop a stable order in which certain patterns of organization repeat endlessly and become 'frozen'. In other conditions (high connectivity, high diversity, intense interaction), the result was disorder in which no pattern becomes discernible. Yet other conditions demonstrate a transitional regime: the networks display a capacity for shifting organization, producing patterns that propagate, grow, split apart and recombine in complex ways that do not repeat themselves, although they may have a qualitatively familiar character (Waldrop, 1992). This behaviour occurred when the parameters influencing the way the network interact reaches certain critical values producing behaviour which paradoxically combines order and disorder at the same time. Complex networks interacting in such conditions were dubbed 'at the edge of chaos' by Langton, since the patterns produced were neither random nor repetitive, but seemed to combine both characteristics simultaneously. Ray's simulations in particular took on a life of their own as the agents were not programmed to follow a single instruction set of interaction rules, but to evolve their own instruction sets as a result of interacting.

In an earlier volume in this series, Stacey (2001: 70–75) describes Ray's simulation Tierra and Stacey uses this as an abstract analogy for the process of life evolving in a self-organizing dynamic. However, Stacey warns us that, as we transfer this analogy of interaction 'at the edge of chaos' to the domain of human interaction, we can have no analogy for the programmer, a point I will return to below (p. 68).

Langton made another analogy by comparing the 'edge of chaos' dynamics of his networks of cellular automata to second order phase transitions between matter in the solid and liquid states. When held at critical levels of temperature and pressure, such phase transitions are not sharp as we normally experience them.

> Slightly above the transition temperature most of the molecules are tumbling over one another in the fluid phase, but amongst them are myriad sub-microscopic islands of orderly lattice solid, with molecules constantly dissolving and re-crystallising around the edges. These islands are neither very big nor very long-lasting, even on a molecular scale. So the system is still mostly chaos. But as the temperature is lowered, the largest islands start to get very big indeed, and they begin to live for a correspondingly long time . . . Of course if the temperature were taken all the way past the transition, the roles would reverse: the material would go from being a sea of fluid dotted with islands of solid, to being a continent of solid dotted with lakes of fluid. But right *at* the transition . . . the ordered structures fill the same volume as the chaotic fluid. Order and chaos intertwine in a complex, ever-changing dance of sub-microscopic arms and fractal filaments. The largest ordered structures propagate their fingers across the material for arbitrarily long distances and arbitrarily long time . . . *And nothing ever really settles down.*
>
> (Waldrop, 1992: 231, my italics)

Notice again that Langton is interested in making an analogy with a laboratory situation in which conditions of temperature and pressure are set and held by the observing scientist. Again there is no 'external agency' in nature setting or holding such conditions steady, just as there is no programmer setting the conditions of interaction as for Ray's simulations. These analogies have to do with the nature of the dynamic 'at the edge of chaos' but not its production. So how does the 'edge of chaos' dynamic offer a metaphor and an analogy for the self-patterning process of human interaction?

As a metaphor we can imagine that in free-flowing communicative action, we co-create qualities of responsiveness between us whereby we experience meaning on the move, neither completely frozen into repetitive patterns nor fragmenting and dissolving into meaninglessness. From within the conduct of the conversation, what seems solid would be melting at the edges, while what seems shapeless would be gaining form, at the same time, not to create a single unified landscape for all, but a shifting topology of partial orderings in which we recreate our situation as both recognizable and potentially novel at the same time.

As an analogy, in this series, we would not be taking an individualist cognitive view of humans whose behaviour in relation to one another is understood by appealing to mental schema, instead we take a relational view of forming and being formed simultaneously in interaction. The 'conditions' that affect the kind of patterning are no longer quantitative parameters which can be set by an external agency. Rather, they are variations in the qualities of human communication to do with such relational factors as the movement of affinity/antipathy, inclusion–exclusion, identity/difference, competition/co-operation, power relating and experiences of anxiety/spontaneity. We can create between us 'conditions' in which we experience our conversations as stuck and repetitive, or more positively, as reassuringly recreating a sense of familiarity and stability. It is also possible for us to create conditions in which we experience loss of meaning and, indeed, alarming experiences of loss of self. However, we also often co-create conditions of free-flowing communication which we experience as the paradox of continuity and change. The significance of the past may be recast, a new sense of where to go from here materializes, there may be a shift in people's sense of self and in their relations to others, what can be envisaged takes on a fresh shape. The patterning of our social identities shifts spontaneously.

Of course, despite emphasizing the spontaneous emergence of this 'edge of chaos' dynamic in conversation, we humans want to produce it more reliably. We want to identify and set the parameters in advance. This is what comes of forgetting that we cannot recreate the role of the programmer, the person who sets and hold the conditions we want, sets up the 'right' rules of engagement. Still we try to step into that role together as we spend time 'in advance' of starting a conversation trying to agree the 'ground rules' for good communication. I have been with many groups coming up with lists like this:

> Do not interrupt one another
> Listen carefully
> Respect others' views
> Suspend judgments
> Express yourself concisely and clearly
> Check your understanding
> Balance support and challenge
> Be open and honest
> and so on . . .

We try to set codified sets of constraints–enablements in the form of idealized rules for individual behaviour that we agree to hold ourselves and one another to. We may find the conduct of the conversation that produces a list like this valuable, but not for reasons that are usually given. Problems arise if we think of the list of rules as either the rules that are actually governing individual behaviour or the rules of interaction that are creating a 'group culture'. If we do so, we are accepting an individual cognitive model of human beings as autonomous rule-following entities as adequate, and we are deluding ourselves that we can delineate a 'system of communication' and condition it as though from outside of it and then subject ourselves to it. We believe we can create ideal conditions that should reliably deliver the experience we tantalizingly know can happen. The trouble is that the different qualities of conversation that we experience as we converse, are precisely that – *qualities*. And, as complexity scientists like Brian Goodwin (1994) point out, qualities are emergent properties of interaction which cannot be analysed in terms of the behaviour of the individual agents or their interaction. Rather, he suggests, we may recognize consensually shifts in our experience of conversation. We may agree that a particular conversation shifts, although there may be conflicting meanings generated in relation to this. The trouble is that our experience of the differing qualities of conversation leads us to formulate notions of 'good conversation' that may be unhelpful.

Key themes

In this chapter I have been describing and accounting for organizational change practice as participation in local communicative action in the living present. Rather than formulating attempts to operate on any kind of whole system or sub-system, I am describing the process of weaving in our actions one with one another to co-create our future. In so doing I am making a number of suggestions for how we might think of such a practice in terms of the transformative activity of conversing:

- that our organizing changes as our patterns of accounting to one another for what we are doing changes.
- that we may understand ourselves as engaged in the co-created, open-ended, never complete activity of jointly constructing our future, not as the realization of a shared vision, but as emerging courses of action that make sense of going on together.
- that such activity that is constructive of the future involves an everyday paradox of subversion that shifts legitimation.
- that we must pay proper attention to this process of prospective sense-making rather than only attempting to piece together a picture of our situation that we may then seek to change.
- that we are shaping and shifting our co-created webs of mutual constraint–enablement in our ongoing interaction rather than attempting to set these constraints–enablements in advance as formative guidelines.
- that the transformative potential of conversation may be blocked by demands for early clarity or closure.
- that acting without clear outcomes in mind does not mean acting randomly without intention.
- that clearly agreed roles are not always needed for useful participation.

I began Chapter 1 by describing how my approach to organizational change practice fails to meet the expectations of the mainstream perspective. In the last chapter and this one I am beginning to show that this is not a personal idiosyncrasy. I am beginning to construct a coherent rationale for such an approach based on understanding organizations as complex responsive processes of relating. I am describing a mode of working that does not proffer a blueprint for practice, that does not define roles or select working models. Rather, I am describing how we may join ongoing conversations as participant sense-makers, helping to develop the opportunities inherent in such conversations. I am suggesting that this involves moving into constraints, restrictions and premature closures as they materialize in communicative action so as to sustain exploratory meaning making. I am drawing attention to vital, informal, shadow processes that more dominant systematic perspectives render rationally invisible. These are the ordinary, everyday processes of organizational life that offer endless opportunity as we move from conversation to conversation.

In the next chapter I will pick up on something that has been implicit throughout these last two chapters. That our participation in creating 'organized settings' of paradoxical enabling constraints means that all our relating can be understood as sustaining and shifting power relations, with all the anxieties that entails. This leads to a particular way of appreciating the politics of organizational life. In Chapter 5, I will pick up another implicit theme and discuss the nature of ensemble improvisation. I will suggest that this analogy from the world of theatre may help us take seriously and develop further our capacity for the ordinary yet considerable craft of constructing our future as communicative interaction.

4 The politics of change

- Self-organizing power figurations
- The dynamics of inclusion–exclusion
- Back in Ferrovia – the lead up to and aftermath of the Site Committee meeting
- The start of another cultural change assignment

Self-organizing power figurations

We are daily involved with others in forming and being formed by the evolving 'situations' which we experience as the sensible interweaving of our actions with one another. I have been describing this in terms of our participation in a self-organizing process of a largely conversational nature. We create 'organized settings' of constraints–enablements that are always evolving as we communicate and which leave behind material and intangible traces in the form of artefacts, codifications and habits of institutionalization. Just because such 'organized settings' do not always exist as literal structures or contexts separate from or outside of our ongoing relating does not make them in any way less *real* for us. Taking seriously the socially-constructed nature of our mutual constraining is to take seriously our living experience of ourselves enmeshed in webs of power relations.

We cannot shake ourselves free of this web for, as the sociologist Norbert Elias (Mennell and Goudsblom, 1998) pointed out, we live as human beings within patterns of interdependencies, which he called 'figurations'. This has important implications for how we understand the paradox of human freedom. Throughout a large part of the twentieth century Elias was quietly pointing out that most sociologists were 'atomists' or 'holists' analysing statistically the behaviour of large numbers of individuals or examining the structures of 'whole societies'. Elias believed that both of these approaches missed investigating how people's actions and experience intermesh in a dynamic patterning process in which the individual and the social arise together. He did not use the terms 'self-organization' or 'emergence' but his thinking was along these same lines. Unlike most sociologists, who see the social as a 'system' at a different level of analysis to the individual 'system', Elias spoke of the person as social through and through and of the *social* being the plural and the *person* being the singular of the same process of relating. We are always, whether in silent imagination or overt communication, relating ourselves to others.

Elias draws attention to power in human affairs in ways that are significantly different from the way power is often discussed in organizations. First, he points out that power is not an attribute or possession of a single person but is characteristic of human relating – power arises between us in our relationships. Second, he points out that *all* relating can be understood as power relating. To sustain a relation to another person is to actively engage in a jointly-created process of mutual constraint that affords each of us opportunities while at the same time limiting us. Elias points out how this is as true for enmity and hostility as it is for friendship and co-operation – these are all forms of mutually sustained relating born of mutual valuing however evenly or unevenly distributed. By 'valuing' Elias meant the way we require certain kinds of responses from others to sustain our sense of self. Others have value for us as they offer, withhold and change their responses to our responses, generating for each of us feelings of being more or less powerful, influential or powerless. It is important to realize that Elias is not describing a rational instrumental process of transactional exchange here. Our relations are creative engagements in which we make our identities as we strive to influence the conditions for going on together. 'I' cannot go on being the same 'me' without continuing to relate to 'you' in a certain way, and if that way shifts we are both a little different.

Further, we are not relating to one person at a time in a series of dyadic encounters but we are relating over time to a 'community' of others without fixed boundaries. The phrase 'power figurations' is used by Elias to evoke the sense of patterning emerging through the dynamic mutual constraining–enabling of one another in our shifting webs of relating. Power figurations are then profoundly historical, social, local communicative processes in which our activities simultaneously perpetuate and potentially transform the patterns which sustain and evolve our joint capacities to act in some ways rather than others. What is more, although we may each be developing political intentions, consciously making bids to influence the course of events, shifts in power figurations occur spontaneously and unpredictably beyond the control of any one party or group, as is the nature of all self-organizing processes.

The dynamics of inclusion–exclusion

Perhaps the most obvious way we experience power relations at work is in the way we are always acting to include and exclude others and experiencing ourselves as included and excluded. When such in–out, inside–outside patterns seem relatively stable we tend to talk of boundaries and the way redrawing the boundaries may change the system. We are employing a spatial metaphor of inclusion–exclusion as ideological categories of membership. Organizations with aspirations for greater social inclusion are always trying to draw in more diversity, widening the boundaries of stakeholder definition and participation, considering positive discrimination to level the mix of membership 'inside and outside' across certain identified boundaries, according to certain agreed dimensions. Concerns on a smaller scale outlaw forms of expression which may exclude or divide, leading to the new oppressions of political correctness which draw ideological boundaries around what can or cannot be said.

In this series we advocate working with exclusion–inclusion as a temporal process of mutual recognition in a paradoxical Hegellian dialectic. Hegel's notion of dialectic has come down to us primarily in terms of thesis–antithesis–synthesis in the Marxist reading of Hegel's thought. However, following Mead's reading of Hegel we invite a perception of every act of exclusion as also a potential invitation to inclusion. This is because further acts may shift the meaning, whereby the original exclusion made sense and vice versa. This may have been what Hegel meant by the idea of 'negating the negation' (see Griffin, 2001, for a fuller exposition of these ideas). Thus, in local interaction the potential to shift the ways we may recognize and feel recognized as persons in social realities arises. Such processes of shifting the specific manifestations of implicit ideologies from within our ongoing experience of power relating may, of course, be highly anxiety provoking and the quality of our participation in mutually reducing such anxiety and sustaining sufficient spontaneity becomes critical.

Let us consider further accounts of organizational change practice informed by this perception of our participation as inevitable and inescapable political processes. As I recount events I will draw attention in italics to the way I experienced this process at work.

Back in Ferrovia – the lead up to and aftermath of the Site Committee meeting

About a year after all the activities I have already described had been underway, the question of the formal management development programme for the plant is progressing ponderously through the agenda of the Regional Government Office. This body was set up to award financial backing to firms offering approved employee training in this still rather undeveloped part of Italy. As is typical of such bodies, it has very conventional expectations of expert taught programmes and Stefano, in charge of management development at the plant, has been busy for months trying to come up with designs that will satisfy their criteria. Much earlier, discussions about this have provided a legitimate reason for returning to Ferrovia to meet with Allesandro and the group of people seen as 'getting it' at the plant.

Since then the actual experience of learning and change at the plant has been influenced by the kind of activities that have emerged in the gatherings and forums that Doug and I have encouraged. Eventually Carlo, the Site Manufacturing Manager convenes a group to discuss the plant's approach to staff and management development.

It is an unusual group, consisting of Carlo, Stefano and his assistant, Doug and myself, Alessandro, Lorenzo, Simona and Walter, all people who have been involved in various sense-making gatherings and their ripple effects. There are also a couple of others, including Bob, seconded from the US and responsible for introducing the new IT management systems into the plant.

Earlier that morning we had drunk a quick coffee with Cesare, the head of quality improvement, who said that he thought Carlo was becoming rejuvenated. 'It is as though he has rediscovered hope,' said Cesare. Certainly he is in lively form this morning. He feels, he says, that a wave of potential is bubbling up through and across the plant. He speaks with feeling about his conviction that the organization is adjusting itself to the new context of the spin-off and that his role as a senior manager is to recognize and move with this. He wants the current proposals in the Training and Development Plan for a series of 'Managing Change' workshops replaced with an attempt to capitalize on the approach Doug and I have introduced. It becomes clear after painstaking circular discussions with Stefano that no such proposal will get a grant from the Regional Government Office.

The design of the programmes is constrained by the policies of the Regional Office which are themselves constrained by the desire of the Government to encourage firms to invest in more staff development. Stefano frets under this but he is constrained from challenging the guidelines by the Site Manager, Giorgio's, need for the enabling extra cash and his desire to continue being recognized by the Government as high on their lists of good employers. Our conversation sustained these interdependencies with little change.

'OK,' says Carlo eventually, sweeping away this impasse, 'we forget about trying to fit this into the formal programme. This will happen alongside that activity, we will just have to ensure that the training sessions are used simply to impart general information to employees.'

In this move power figurations shift as a whole set of activities are no longer included as part of Stefano's area of responsibility. He looks relieved as he sustains his existing identity in relation to negotiations with the Regional Office, although he becomes less included in the conversations which follow.

Carlo now wants to create a 'design team' from members of this group to think through a development process to discuss with the Site Committee. He imagines gathering some of the people already spontaneously involved with the initiatives Doug and I have helped to spawn, adding in more from areas not yet involved. We will help them become a population of change agents that reaches into every corner of the plant, with the remit to identify the themes and issues of change in Ferrovia. The members of this group will then be asked to convene other groupings over a three-month period to discuss and work on these issues. In this way the population of managers and staff who are presently the target of the 'Managing Change' programmes will also participate in a much livelier and more relevant development that will be part of the actual process of change. He pauses and smiles around, expecting a warm reception for his proposals.

A new 'entity' – the design team – is emerging which will create new relationships between its members, with the Site Committee members and with other people in the plant. Doug and I would immediately experience a shift towards a greater formalization of our involvement with different constraints–enablements.

I experience mixed feelings. It is true that the plan Carlo is suggesting is much more interesting than the standard proposals which are rolling ponderously through the procedures at the Regional Government offices. Carlo is also recognizing that, from the very active encouragement of different kinds of open-ended conversation at Ferrovia, has come some different patterns of working and that these *are* the changes in working culture that he and his colleagues keep trying to establish how to identify and create. But the irregular, uneven, unexpected nature of our work, which has allowed much to happen rather quickly, is about to be lost in the attempt to try to turn this into a systematic and ordered approach. I wonder to myself about the timing of this.

The shift for Lorenzo and his colleagues would also be considerable, something Lorenzo is immediately alive to.

To Carlo's obvious surprise, Lorenzo is immediately uncomfortable. 'But you will create a special group who are cut off from their peers, labelled formally as "change agents" and who will immediately be seen as part of formal management or as a cadre of special people. It will change the spirit of what we are doing!' 'But,' says Carlo, 'I am offering you the opportunity to be a major influence in the evolution of the plant.' Lorenzo is visibly upset in his vain struggle to make Carlo see the possible futility of this offer from his point of view. He already feels like a major influence and being included in this meeting has increased that. Carlo seems bemused.

Carlo can offer Lorenzo more formal authority but he needs him to want it. He is less aware of Lorenzo's sense of himself as a leader amongst his own peers which his offer puts at risk. Lorenzo, on the other hand, feels that a move to include him more in management acivities will exclude him more in the networks of the plant and he may feel less influential.

As the conversation continues, different themes start to emerge. Carlo is genuinely excited by what is beginning to shift at the plant. He is not so single minded that he does not realize that there can be no simple tracing of cause and effect, but he understands that the approach Doug and I are taking is contributing to the process of change and he very much wants us to continue. However, he feels that the success of the work in stirring unexpected networks and conversations into life is disturbing the status quo of the Site Committee, who have worked together over decades in most cases, and who share a perception of change directed and led systematically from the top. He feels now is the moment to bring a discussion about what is happening to this management forum.

The growing relationships between Doug, myself, Carlo and Cesare and between Carlo and various people involved in the networks have disturbed the patterning of power relations in the Site Committee. Carlo believes some feel excluded from activities that are having an impact and he wants to include them more.

As this theme evolves in our conversation, Carlo and Lorenzo begin to talk more about what it might mean for there to be 'a sea-change' in the Site Committee's understanding of their part in the process of change – that they might 'bless' what is stirring around them. 'What I want,' says Carlo finally, 'is for an open-ended conversation like this to take place with the Site Committee. I want this kind of experience to occur there so that all the senior managers *know* what we mean by self-organizing change and can notice differently and participate differently in what is happening.' So we agree that a meeting of the 'design team' and the Site Committee will take place. It was, as usual, interesting to note that the very considerable sense of energy and purpose at the end of the meeting seemed related to our having created broad ways to go forward rather than very specific objectives about where all this will lead.

The meeting is convened in early June. Carlo has booked the larger conference room in the Dirigenti building. An enormous table occupies it so that the eighteen of us are pressed around the walls with this large dead wooden space connecting/separating us. There is nothing to be done about this; the table is immovable and the other meeting room too small. This is, after all, a formal meeting with the full Site Committee, although the membership is unique for such an occasion. Bob is working with an American colleague who was intrigued when he told her about the meeting he was about to attend. Since she is professionally interested in organizational change, she asked if she could join him. Simona and Lorenzo had wanted Louisa to be there, but she had been reluctant, saying her English was not up to it. Alessandro had been developing a rapport with Roberto, one of the two managers in charge of the research labs, and like Eduardo, the other senior lab manager, a member of the Site Committee. Alessandro had told Roberto of Louisa's part in the emergence of the luncheon initiatives. It was Roberto who personally went and persuaded Louisa, on the morning of the meeting, that her contribution was needed. Alessandro himself was unable to attend, but

Piero who had initially been so reluctant to make any visible move was there, as were Cesare, and Franco, who had been involved in the film business conversational sessions, both of them also members of the Site Committee. So, although Carlo had spoken of the groundswell of activity that had occurred in the plant, as though 'bottom up', in fact those who had become involved held positions throughout the hierarchy of the plant.

It was very unusual for this leadership group to include others in their meetings in this way. Usually people were invited in ones and twos to provide requested presentations and then left. Even when Doug and I first came to visit this team a year ago and sat down to converse with them rather than present to them, we were treated and responded very much as their 'guests'. Here no one person was responsible for the inclusion of all the 'extras'. This situation, with nearly as many non-members as members of the Site Committee present together for an open-ended conversation was a new experience. The 'host–guest' or the 'royalty requiring report from underling' form of relating could not be sustained between us. This meant we had a grouping where the identities of everyone in relation to one another was more than usually uncertain and open to movement.

Carlo introduces the meeting by saying that he hopes for an opportunity to discuss the leadership of change in the plant. Around the table sit those with formal roles as the leadership of the plant and also those who are taking up a more spontaneous form of leadership by initiating networks of communication within and beyond the site. This is a chance to reach mutual understanding and explore ways forward, particularly in linking this to the way the plant approaches formal staff and management development.

Usually Giorgio would have led all Site Committee meetings, but it seemed 'natural' to us all that this role moved to Carlo on this occasion.

Carlo indicates that he is offering Lorenzo the chance to speak. It was clear to me that Lorenzo had prepared himself for this. 'First of all,' he says, 'I would like to suggest we follow the innovation that Doug and Patricia have introduced of speaking in a mixture of Italian and English, rather than insisting on English. This allows everyone to express themselves freely.' I feel the surprise in the American woman sitting next to me. 'But I won't understand,' she whispers to me. I say she might be surprised and anyway this meeting is about shifting something important in the plant, our exact comprehension is less important than the Italians' need for subtlety and flexibility of expression in a rather ambiguous situation.

The use of language always influences the constraints–enablements of international meetings, shifting the degree of inclusion–exclusion. Allowing the messy flow between different languages increases the potential for movement of webs of power relating. Different people experience different degrees of inclusion and exclusion as the use of language shifts. This is, of course, as true for different professional discourses as it is for national languages. Instinctively Lorenzo moves to include himself more by his suggestion and links himself firmly to Doug and myself by suggesting this as an innovation rather than a weakness in his English.

At this point Lorenzo switches into Italian, speaking slowly. Listening and watching attentively I know that he is recounting what has been happening at the plant from his perspective. Fulvio interrupts him and there is a quicker exchange between him and Lorenzo. I ask what the key point is here and Carlo explains that some of the managers are concerned that the people involved in these activities are concentrated in clusters. They do not extend to all sectors of the plant. Why is this? It means that the groups are not representative. Before I have a chance to say anything, Louisa replies in Italian with some vehemence, soon joined by Lorenzo. This time I understand that they are making two points. First, that the very visible network of people most involved with us is only a small part of the networks of people in communication with one another right across the plant. And second, the patchiness is because the networks have emerged spontaneously, without any central decision. 'Well,' said Roberto, 'maybe this is the time to take action to even things out more.' Piero agrees with this, evoking an even more passionate spate of Italian from Louisa and Lorenzo.

I come in to tell in more detail the story of how Doug and I had first visited the plant a year ago because we had called Carlo, whom we knew. I recount the mixture of intention and chance by which events have evolved. I explain that we have often arrived at the plant with perhaps two pre-planned appointments at most, and then found opportunities for many other conversations, moving quickly into whatever possibilities arose to take things further with other people, often with no end goal in mind. As I hoped, my tale provokes further stories from others about what has flowed from the many encounters that have taken place, eventually creating activities that have become visible in the life of the plant. I notice that

Franco and Cesare are surprisingly quiet although they know a lot about what has happened. I feel the quickening of interest in Roberto who is sitting on the other side of me. He encourages further conversation about how all this is creating a sense of 'the culture' shifting in important ways. What further changes might be possible? His questions are asked in a tone of real curiosity, so that again there is about 15 minutes of Italian exchanges. Nearly an hour and a half have passed. Carlo says that we might discuss how to proceed with this work alongside more formal development activities. He looks at Eduardo who has been completely silent up to this point. 'What do you think, Eduardo?'

This animated conversation has created a particular sense of what has been happening at the plant, fashioned afresh from the contributions of those present. The telling between us creates its own momentum for going forward. Carlo feels this is the moment to invite someone who has not been very supportive of our activities to weave themselves into the possibilities we are constructing.

Eduardo raises his head deliberately and an extraordinary expectant hush fills the room. He speaks in Italian, slowly, and I understand every word. 'I have nothing to say in this situation. I suggest that the consultants and other extraneous parties be asked to leave the room so that the Site Committee members can continue discussion in private.' Silence with the weight of lead seems to have settled round the table. In a flash I notice Cesare's eyes fixed on his hands, Roberto sighing and shaking his head, a sharp intake of breath from the American woman beside me. Everyone is avoiding eye contact with everyone else.

Eduardo's instincts are to try to sustain the power relations he is familiar and comfortable with. This means trying to recreate the dynamic of the Site Committee rather than contribute to this discussion – no matter what he actually wants to say. The new patterning of the interactions of the last hour and a half are too fragile to sustain themselves in the face of Eduardo's reconfiguring of the group as 'we' and 'extraneous' others. It is as though people find themselves immediately responding in habitual ways to his own habitual response.

I find I am already speaking before I even realize it: 'Eduardo, I think you have suggested that I and others leave the room, but I think it would be much better if you could say something of what you think while we are here.' Eduardo glares at me and says nothing. I remember my earlier impression of a very introverted man and I try again. 'There has been a dramatic response to what you said and how you said it. I feel as though I am walking on a precipice in continuing to try and talk to you.' Eduardo continues to say nothing, but removes his glasses and folds them up. I hear Carlo speaking, the nervousness in his voice unmistakable. He babbles something about a useful exchange. Allowing time for assimilation. Further discussion will be needed. . . . The meeting breaks up with alacrity, people seem desperate to get out of the room.

Doug and I exchange a few words. We are both amazed at the sudden and unexpected fragmentation of the meeting. The frozen atmosphere that had been created in the room is in sharp contrast to the surge of energy that is exploding now as people scatter into twos and threes. Doug and I hang around. Piero is disappearing through the front door, reminding me of an agitated white rabbit, perhaps with his worst fears confirmed. We see Lorenzo and Louisa in intense conversation with Carlo. Cesare approaches us, beside himself with delight. For him the afternoon has demonstrated in a very public way the 'no-go' wall he has felt himself come up against over and over again in his attempts to get the full support of the Site Committee for his work to improve quality. Giorgio, the Site Manager, appears and asks in urgent tones if Doug and I would step into his office for a moment. None of us sits down. Giorgio says, 'This was a difficult meeting, but also good, very good. We want you to continue. It is very important you continue.' Doug and I say something about the difficulty that everyone seemed to have in continuing after Eduardo's comments. Giorgio looks exhausted. 'Eduardo is a very respected and important member of the team.' I say:

> This is not about Eduardo, alone. We responded to one another in that
> room in a way that created a fearful vice that strangled conversation.
> It was almost impossible to speak and it was such a relief to break up,
> but we are all implicated in this. It is the repeated experience of this
> that feeds the perception that Ferrovia is unable to change, which we
> know is far from true.

Giorgio replies, 'Yes, but something very different has happened now – although I can't say exactly . . .'

Outside Giorgio's office, we meet Carlo. In the middle of the reception area we have a passionate exchange. 'Carlo,' I say, 'it was almost as if you actually invited Eduardo to do what he did. Why? You kind of knew what was coming?' Carlo was more sombre than I had ever seen him. 'I don't know,' he replies, 'but something may come of this. I don't know.'

Doug and I retire to our rooms in the guest house and open a bottle of wine. We are tired and yet somehow satisfied, disturbed, agitated and confident all at the same time. We both feel as though events are moving fast in ways we cannot begin to grasp but which feels at least significant.

What I am describing here is the complex self-organizing process in which emerging power figurations are patterning communicative action as continuity and potential transformation of those power figurations. The patterning arises in the continuous circling of gesture and response, of turn-taking and turn making, of including and excluding, of mutual accounting, of the shifts in enabling–constraints, of expectation, privilege, obligation and entitlement by which people relate to one another. Narrative and propositional themes are arising as associated but differing experiences for each person repatterning in the present the experience of social identity. Although each person may be aware of conscious intentions, aspirations, fears and desires that move them as they act, there are also less conscious 'tendencies of feelings' and imaginative elaborations weaving together in the cooperative–conflictual communicative process. These processes which we may each experience as sometimes enlivening, sometimes deadening, anxiety provoking and exciting are the very stuff of organizational and communal life. They are inescapable yet, rather than pay attention to our ongoing involvement in this process, we tend in organizations to promote idealized models of conflict management and change management. I fear that this does little to help us reflect on the continuously emerging issues of ethics and integrity that arise between us in our organizing.

Only one week later back in England we receive a fax from Carlo: 'I'm suggesting that we try to be available to meet on Monday 23rd June at 8.15 a.m. in Giorgio's office. We will discuss how to define and implement the activities of several working groups. I'm looking forward to seeing you.'

Compared to the last occasion, the mood in Giorgio's office is like walking into the temperate zone after a spell in the hothouse at Kew Gardens. In their view the tumultuous meeting has been a watershed. It has been followed by a number of conversations between Carlo, Giorgio, Roberto and Eduardo. There is a new understanding and support for our work. The 'blessing' that Carlo had wanted has apparently been achieved. There will be no attempt to systematize what we were doing; there will instead be recognition that people are becoming involved in an unpredictable way with various initiatives and the managers will make it clear that this is welcomed and will participate themselves as much as possible. It was clear that something significant had shifted in the dynamic of the Site Committee, there was a new alliance between Eduardo and Roberto in which Eduardo's attitude to many things seemed to have softened and Roberto appeared quite statesman-like in ways that had not been apparent before. Giorgio talked openly of wanting to take early retirement and there seemed a confident expectation that Carlo would become the next Site Manager. Lorenzo was no longer bothered about the idea of a population of change agents now that it was not to be given a management remit and said that people were feeling very differently towards Eduardo, no less respect but less fear.

We have a further meeting with a group of the 'change agent' population in July. This group has continued to grow. They seem to know exactly what they want to do. They have contacted the person responsible for employee communication on the site and are going to discuss with him some unusual material they want published – simple messages and cartoons without explanation that they believe will strike a chord in the plant and stimulate discussion. They intend to put posters up around the canteens and convene an open forum to create some cross-functional groups to generate and take forward ideas. There seems to be plenty of energy and confidence for moving forward and Doug and I feel that we should leave them to it, keeping in touch with interest and for the sake of the relationships which we have formed with many of the people we have come to know. I recognize that the initiative is now taking a form somewhat similar to the 100 Forum that developed at the Boroughsville assignment which I have described in an earlier paper (Shaw, 1997). There, too, there had been an unpredictable shift in the patterns of mutual constraint and what had been viewed as rather subversive activity became increasingly accepted as a legitimate way to work.

This story tells of power shifts of an obvious and rather dramatic kind, but it is important to recognize that what I want to draw attention to is occurring all the time in very ordinary, everyday ways. Take, for example, the way the whole assignment with this spin-off company began and how a 'contract' for working with change in the company arose.

The start of another cultural change assignment

I return to my home office one day in early April, to find three messages on my answer machine, all from the same company. The first is from a woman with a German accent, reminding me that we met a couple of years ago during a session on cross-cultural teamwork for a division of an American owned multinational. I know that a decision to create a 'spin-off' company was announced during the previous autumn. The move sent shock waves through the company as some 8000 people were faced with a compulsory change in employment. The sheer size and diversity of the corporation's operations throughout the world, and its benevolent 'family' values had made life-long job security seem guaranteed. Since then there has been a wave of redundancies, mostly voluntary, but not entirely. Also employees who suddenly found themselves part of the new spin-off organization are banned from reapplying to the parent company for two years.

Over a period of some months, the multinational has been ejecting a cluster of related businesses and disentangling the financial and administrative processes that bind these to the parent company. The new company is due to become a distinct formal and legal entity on 1st July.

The tone of the message from Greta, the woman in Germany, is excited and urgent. She is putting together a team of external consultants to help develop and lead some sessions throughout Europe 'to help create the new culture of WhatCo', as the spin-off company has been temporarily dubbed. She wants me to join this venture, along with a German and a Danish consultant, both of whom I have worked with before.

The second message is from a man with a French accent, introducing himself as Alex, the head of HR for WhatCo in Europe. He wants to speak to me about developing the new company. I am not sure whether we have met before or not. I do not recognize his name or his voice. The third message is spoken in rather languid, ironic English tones that I know quite well. They belong to Donald, WhatCo's recently appointed Managing Director, Operations in Europe, whom I have worked with on and off over a period of some 10 years as he moved through a succession of promotions in the late stages of a successful career:

> Ah, Patricia. We have a few goings on here as you are probably aware. We're up to our eyeballs in the transition to WhatCo and I've just been speaking with a chappie from the Management Consultant outfit we're paying a small fortune to, about culture change. Gerry was with me (remember Gerry?) and after an hour with this guy, we were unimpressed. We think you have more understanding about culture in your little finger and maybe you won't cost the arm and a leg that this fellow is suggesting. So we'd like you on board. You'll probably get a phone call from Alex, our new HR guy.

I smile as I listen to this. I am familiar with the ambiguous mix of flattery and laconic challenge that had, at first, made me uneasy working with Donald. I have come to like him, thinking of him as a wily old bird, whom I respect for his business sense and thoughtfulness about the complexities of leadership and warm to for the infectious humour he brings to his job. In the past, working with him has always been demanding and stimulating.

These three voices call forth immediate responses from me. I move through a whole series of sensations and feelings: pleasurable anticipation, discomfort, fleeting memories, attraction and reluctance. I experience anew my sense of rapport with Donald, complex unease about some aspects of my memories of working with Greta, which I am unable to pin down, a whole cascade of transient responses to the sound of a French accent that I connect with images from my childhood days in France. Immediately I am politically engaged, whatever I do next.

I follow the unease, the thread whose meaning is least clear to me. I decide to call Greta back first. Greta explains that there has already been a series of 'Planning for Success' workshops in every Region. Groups of employees have been asked to brainstorm the changes in culture that are needed as the new company leaves the corporate fold. They have also been asked for the ten best ideas in each Region for building a successful future. She has been involved in these sessions because of her Organization Development role, and thinks that they have gone very well. The material generated is being typed up, summarized and collated across all the Regions by the central WhatCo transition team.

My heart sinks as I listen to this. I can imagine that the experience of these sessions was very helpful in all the uncertainty of the spin-off – another chance to 'make sense'. However I hear the usual reification of culture, anxiety about open spaces, the decision to design in advance the form the sense-making will take – new 'rules' for a new culture, ten best ideas for making a successful new company. I wonder what they will now do with all this 'output' as it becomes increasingly abstracted from the contexts in which it has been generated.

Greta continues:

> Of course, we know there is a problem about creating this new culture as we carry over all the people and habits of the existing corporation with us. That is why I have suggested that we run a series of workshops to be attended by all managers before the official launch of

the new company. I came up with the idea of focusing on the question, 'What happens when the customer calls on July 1st?' This is something Donald has also been asking as he goes round talking with employees. I believe we should aim to deliver a new corporate identity as we speak to people on the phone all over Europe on that day.

I feel increasingly bemused as I listen. I can resonate with the image of people evolving the patterns of the new company as they talk with others, but everyone together, on one day, 'delivering a new corporate identity on the phone'? Why is Greta talking to me about this? I have been quiet for a long time as Greta has been telling me the story so far, and I can feel my silence provoking a stronger desire to persuade in her voice. I feel I must act to stem the tide, as she already senses I am uneasy.

I begin to voice my hesitations and disagreements, but she brushes them aside. No, no, I have not understood. This is to be a major initiative to create the new company:

> to shift people's minds, motivation and attitude. The way they answer the phone will be the visible result of the first but magic step into a new culture. The project will be implemented top-down. I have the support of Donald and Alex, and I have already spoken with Daniella and Gertrude (the other two external consultants) and they have agreed enthusiastically.

I feel the pressure to go along with her, her conviction, passion and sincerity. I am being asked to join an enterprise that is already well underway. I want time to think. I say that I am not sure that this is a project I can usefully contribute to. I imagine puzzlement, a slight withdrawal in the short pause that follows. She has made an offer expecting me to accept it at least provisionally. She has sought to move and persuade me, appeal in a range of ways, not as a set of consciously chosen strategies but in the ordinary way of conversing. I have responded in a way that breaks the flow of our going on together. I start to form the words that will sustain our relating.

'Look, Greta,' I say, 'I have to be honest and tell you that this doesn't really make sense to me yet, I would like to better understand the thinking behind this initiative.' I hear her faint relief. No problem, she will fax through some papers that afternoon.

I can feel some tension in my stomach as I put down the phone. I am already playing a small part in the conversations in which events are evolving and in which I may be included or excluded. I have significant working relationships with many people in this firm and that history of relating is shaping and colouring my reactions as my mind and pulse races. I recall the eagerness in Greta's voice – no doubt this project is a significant one for her. She has pulled in an existing set of collegial relations amongst the external consultants she wants to employ, no doubt thinking that this will speed the design and implementation of her ideas. I forgot to ask whether Donald has already suggested to her that he would like to see me involved. Does Donald know about this proposal? Clearly, yes. Greta was at pains to point out that he was backing her.

I decide to wait until I receive the faxed information. This includes a letter addressed 'Dear consultants' and copies of some messages that have passed between Greta and others by electronic mail. Here are some extracts from the letter:

> Employees want WhatCo to become famous among customers as quickly as possible. Employees will bring across to customers that we are a company that takes care of them, we are responding quickly, with a high degree of quality, we are close to them, we offer as quickly as possible solutions to their problems, we offer total service around them. They are the centre of all we do. Employees want that we appear to customers in a similar way all over the world. A kind of uniformity.

> We have set up a task force 'Corporate Identity via the phone'. On 2nd of May I will give a presentation to the global HR/OD team on this project. In June all workshops will take place in Italy, France, Benelux, Scandinavia, UK, Spain, Germany and Central Region.

> ● On July 1st we will see the results: All employees (that means top-down) will transfer the Corporate Identity via the phone. They will sound, appear and behave like they are by then: highly motivated to guarantee from their function WhatCo's success and to bring across all the things they mentioned in the Planning for Success workshops.

Even accounting for the way the German language produces the imperative mood when English is used, I am astonished by this document. If this is a sample of what is afoot in WhatCo, then I can only imagine that there are some very nervous people around, thinking that something must be done in a big way to manage the uncertainties inherent in the situation. The memo speaks of culture change as a major internal PR exercise, getting everyone to march in step into a brave new future. Yet when I had spoken with Greta I sensed that she was advocating activity that she genuinely believed would generate lasting change – 'a magic step into a new culture' – the phrase was telling.

I turn to the other background information. Greta has sent notes to key people – Donald, Alex, Heinrich, her boss (Manager of European Field Service Operations) and Gerry (leading the Transition Team, responsible for making sure everything is ready for the launch day). She has positioned her suggestions as evolving naturally from what employees have said during the Planning for Success workshops. She has sent me copies of the managers' responses:

> Sounds good. Well done. Donald.

> I think it's a very good initiative. It would be good leverage to go European right from the start, in other words make sure that whatever you come up with is implementable throughout Europe. Alex.

Is it possible, I wonder, that I'm the only one with severe doubts about the value of this kind of activity? I hesitate for a few moments, not sure what I might say, and pick up the phone to dial Gertrude, the German consultant I had worked with before. It is clear that she is very keen on the project. She sees this as a useful way to start working with the new company which will no doubt lead to less constrained opportunities. She is sure that we can come up with some creative ways of working with the brief. If I have reservations, it would be even more valuable to have me in the team to ensure these views are incorporated. In part our conversation is an attempt to make meaning of the invitation in a way that would reassure us that we can include ourselves in the endeavour, despite initial reservations.

After this I sit for a while, slightly agitated, aware of a temptation to claim to be unavailable in the time-scales being proposed. I am becoming enmeshed already in the interplay of mutual influence, always only partly articulated, by which an initiative is emerging, forming, being named, creating alliances and oppositions, attracting support and resources as people talk with each other. I could participate no further or, if I view the emerging proposal as still open to further evolution, I could continue to engage with what is happening. Although I have no formal contract, I am already working, as I understand the term. I am probing, searching to discover what kind of project I might play a part in shaping.

Typically at this stage, a consultant might talk about meeting the sponsoring client to hear the presenting situation and to agree the purpose, goals, terms and conditions of the proposed consulting assignment. Instead I am more interested in adding my voice to the web of conversations sustaining the initiative that is taking shape, so that the meanings evolving in it might continue to move. I know that the conversations I have already had with Greta and with Gertrude have touched off in both of them some reactions whose consequences I cannot know. By declaring myself uneasy with what is being proposed, I have not amplified or reinforced the existing patterns of thinking, but I do not know how significant this difference may be.

In this spirit of probing the stability or otherwise of the emerging activity I call Donald. I pick up the phone at just the point when some sense of purpose is rising in me, but before its exact nature has become clear. I dial the number Donald left on the answer machine and get through immediately. I tell him of Greta's invitation to join the team she is forming, and my surprise that the company is about to embark on this kind of programme.

He sighs and says: 'I've had my doubts, but Greta is very keen to do all this stuff and I don't like to dampen her enthusiasm. We need to generate all the enthusiasm we can get.'

I reply: 'I have seen no sign that anyone is questioning the proposal. You and Alex seem to have given your formal support to her suggested initiatives, so that there is a gathering momentum.'

'Yes, well, her boss in Germany is right behind her and is trying to position her for a European job within the Service operation. Anyway, I wanted you to speak to Alex about the development of WhatCo culture, I wasn't thinking of Greta's project.'

'However, Greta and others are seeing this project as an attempt to create a new culture. Remember the "Growing Together" initiative of a few years ago? What kind of impact did that have?'

Snort from Donald.

I say: 'How different is this from one of those programmes typical of the corporate organization? Yet it is meant to be about signalling a major shift in culture.'

'OK. OK. I get your point. Talk to Alex, will you?'

In these exchanges between us, I voice doubts and stir some response in Donald that seems like vague but non-committal agreement. By associating this initiative with other top-down programmes in the past, I know I am inviting him to recall how irritated he was then as a manager expected to implement them. In reminding him of this he possibly feels slightly cornered. I feel I have touched a nerve but, at the same time, maybe Donald feels irritated by the way I am dwelling on Greta's project.

(In pointing to the possible detail of mutual response going on here I want to emphasize again that all this is not a planned campaign on either part but is emerging between us. It is ordinary, inescapably political relating in which we are shifting between us all the time the enabling constraints within which our communicative actions fit in with one another.)

I call Alex. Apparently, Alex and I have met before. He reminds me of an occasion when I have 'dealt with' a notorious Italian with a reputation for bulldozing discussions. It is on the basis of this that he has responded warmly to Donald's suggestion that he get in touch with me. I dimly remember this incident, but I had no idea of the impression I had made on Alex. I tell him that I have spoken with Greta, Gertrude and Donald and have many questions about the initiative being proposed. Again I feel a pause on the line. It is Alex apparently who has suggested to Greta that she contact me to join the project. He says he also is uncertain about the wisdom of it. As he speaks, I wonder if the real issue for everyone is the challenge of not knowing what action to take in the face of the oft-repeated pressure to create a new culture quickly in order for the new company to succeed. Since the businesses were not making adequate profits to satisfy Wall Street financial analysts within the existing corporation, WhatCo needs to become different, fast. There are new business models, new blueprints and initial strategies, but no one knows how to 'become a different kind of culture'. Cascades of programmes were the well-worn route that the corporation had regularly chosen to enter such terrain in the past, so I am not surprised that this is the kind of suggestion that is calming people's nerves now. But I also know that there is also much historical dissatisfaction with these approaches and I am aware that speaking my doubts is touching this. The difficulty seems to be the idea that the desired 'newness' has to be determined, agreed and implemented, quickly. I ask Alex if he believes that this is how 'newness' develops in practice? 'No,' he says bluntly, 'I don't, but what else can we do?' I don't have a clear sense of what else to do in the sense of a programme of activity, but I suggest that we discuss this further. Since Alex is going to be in the UK in a few days' time, we arrange to meet and talk.

At the end of the week I drive over to the UK office of Mainline, where Alex has suggested we meet. He isn't there; a secretary tells me that his plane has been cancelled and he is unable to travel that day. Thrown off the path I was on by this chance event, I ask if I can use an empty office to make some calls. I sit and look at the phone wondering who I might call, what thread I might pick up. I remember that Donald had mentioned Gerry's name in his telephone call to me, as had Greta, so I ask for the internal directory and dial Gerry's number. I explain why I am at the office and ask if he could make time to talk. 'Stay where you are,' he says, 'I'll be over in five minutes.'

I ask Gerry about his view of Greta's initiative without saying anything about it first. However I am aware that I am probably indicating in many subtle ways my hesitation about it. Here is another person who now says that he is very doubtful, more than doubtful. He thinks it is a disastrous idea, belongs to the old corporate way of thinking and ought to be stopped. Has he tried to argue against it? Well, no. He is hoping it will just die. He is more concerned with his own ideas, as head of the 'transition team' about how to 'launch' the new organization on 1st July. He wants some unexpected things to happen that day to mark a clear divide between the past and the future, like hiring magicians or conjurors or jugglers to wander round the offices. Or maybe he can arrange for some unexpected and funny messages to flash on every computer screen during the morning. Perhaps every location should be encouraged to celebrate with a party. I notice the desire for a 'trick', a waving of a magic wand to change the corporate Cinderella into a bright and successful princess overnight. As it happens, he is expecting to meet with Donald and Alex on Monday. I say I will join the three of them. I do not seek approval for this, but take advantage of the messy situation to include myself.

On Monday I meet Gerry, Alex and Donald for an hour. I do not try to account for my presence but simply join the conversation that begins. Maybe everyone assumes someone else invited me. The spin-off has created the opportunity to shed considerable operating costs in terms of numbers of employees and cumbersome structures so that cash generation will automatically improve in the short term, but then what? The company will need to explore the emerging digital arena to compete; this will mean acquisitions and some radical shifts in the way the business is managed and the relations with the market. The release from the big corporate fold, despite some resentment, anxiety and grief aroused by feelings of being kicked out of the nest, is also an exciting period of 'free fall' or 'take off' in which people are discovering new freedoms of thought and action. The idea exercising Donald is that somehow the 'plane must not land' – how to encourage people to accept the new turbulence and openness as a way of working and not a temporary aberration. Only that way, he feels, will new structures develop quickly enough.

This is a way of speaking that excites me. At this point I talk about my interest in the concept of 'edge of chaos' conditions in which a complex network paradoxically experiences both stability and instability – where variations in the reproduction of existing patterns may amplify to generate real novelty. I talk about how such self-organizing emergence is intrinsically uncontrollable in the usual sense and unpredictable in the longer term. I said that I was interested in working with the self-organizing processes far from certainty and agreement where people really did not and could not know precisely what they were doing, as they acted into an evolving situation. I mention that my concern about the 'corporate identity' programmes is that this is focusing on a shared homogeneous corporate identity to be agreed upon and implemented. I suggest this is a way of thinking which might work for the design of the company logo, but which is completely inappropriate for fostering the spontaneous emergence of new patterns of meaning. This requires difference, not homogeneity in the way people are trying to make sense together of their new situation. As I speak about these ideas Donald lights up – clearly his imagination is caught. 'Exactly, exactly. This is what is happening. This is what we need. I keep trying to say to people – this uncertainty is IT! This is what I mean by not letting the plane land!' Alex and Gerry smile, caught up in the wave of energy that emanates from Donald. 'So you will help us with this.' Donald's tone is more statement than question. This is what he wanted anyway, remembering his message on the answerphone, but the rationale is now falling into place. 'Write something down, brief please.' I say I will draw up a one page offer about how I propose to work with WhatCo.

'What about the "Corporate Identity via the phone" initiative? Will you continue with that at the same time?' I ask. There is an uncomfortable pause. 'Alex, you need to speak with Greta,' Donald says. 'I think she does an excellent job in management training in Germany, but I don't think she should be let loose on organization development at this point.' I wince inwardly. I know that in pursuing my own convictions and in trying to secure conditions in which I can work in ways that make sense to me, I have played a role in changing Greta's immediate fortunes. I have not intended this as a political act, but my participation has dampened one kind of activity and amplified the seeds of another.

Apparently Greta's potential role in the company has already been a subject of discussion on several occasions. Only Heinrich, her boss, is pushing for an expanded role beyond the German region. I say, 'None of you seem to have expressed any doubts to Greta, about her proposal. You encouraged her to continue, yet once I began to talk about my reservations you all claim to have had doubts.' Alex says apologetically that Greta has been very unwell, it was important not to demotivate her. Gerry says nothing. Donald sighs. 'Did we have doubts, or do we recognize now that we had something we can call doubts? I was uneasy, certainly. Anyway, this is what I'm willing to pay you for.' He glared at me with an expression in which I read appreciation, bluff and a mute appeal to tread no harder on the sore spot we had exposed. I felt acutely alive at that moment to the webs of conflicting feelings in which so-called rational decisions are made – self-protection, honesty, concern, anxiety, hope, determination. We ended the meeting.

On my return home I speak with my colleague, Doug Griffin, on the phone, as I want him to share the assignment with me. I write the one page that will serve as the contract for the project, sending copies to Donald, Gerry, Alex and Doug.

I know that Alex is going to speak to Greta about putting a halt to the other initiative, so after a couple of days I call her to talk through what has happened. She is bemused and disappointed. I say that I have acted from my own convictions about what will constitute effective work, and I am aware that one consequence of this has been that vague and unarticulated doubts surrounding her proposal have taken shape in a particular way. 'But they all seemed to support the idea,' she said. 'Yes, I know,' I said. I continued:

> I believe that people do not really know what to do and are therefore flowing with one, then another suggestion as the sense of a complex context shifts. They weren't entirely comfortable but the discomfort was not clear enough to be articulated, so the best thing was to keep going, in order to learn more. I don't think one should attribute in hindsight any false intentions. The sense that is now carrying our actions wasn't there before, waiting to surface. We have constructed it together in recent conversations. Your initiative has set off a train of activity, which has included stimulating me to say some things that have resonated with three people who have the formal authority to support or not an official initiative. I have not planned to stop your initiative; I have been acting in my own interest to try to create conditions in which I feel confident to work. This is not a carefully

planned campaign to undermine you, although it may feel that way.
In fact you are as much a part of the unpredictable chain of events as
I am.

'So,' she asks carefully, 'are you willing to work with me?' 'Yes, of
course,' I say, 'I'll send you copies of the documents I've circulated and
let us try to meet and talk about what you want to do and what I want
to do.'

This emphasis on the political nature of all communicative action is
uncomfortable from the perspective that would see participation in
political activity as a choice one can make. I am insisting that to claim to
be apolitical in human affairs makes as little sense as to claim to be able
to take up a position outside interaction. It is also uncomfortable as the
patterns of enabling constraints which we form in our interaction and
which form us at the same time, are conserved and changed
spontaneously. Indeed in the ordinary relating of everyday life in
organizations people may be constantly dismayed as much as pleased by
the way they may perceive themselves, or be perceived by others, to have
made a difference to the evolution of meaning.

We are always trying to place ourselves apart from the communicative
processes which are our experience of living, *as if* we could survey the
patterning of relationship from outside the process of relating. We try to
analyse and choose the part we are playing in an interaction whose
overall shape we try to grasp. Whenever we do this we are identifying the
most repetitive and so apparently stabilized aspects of our relating,
treating this as a puzzle or 'game' we can solve or manage. Whenever we
do this, we are shifting our attention away from the messy experience of
living within the shifting sands of interdependence where we experience
ourselves paradoxically as free and constrained at the same time. We
know we can potentially make a difference but we cannot know in
advance of our acting how the emerging meaning of that difference will
continue to develop. As elaborated by Doug Griffin in an earlier volume
in this series (Griffin: 2001) recognizing the self-organizing nature of our
social participation has profound implications for how we might
reconsider the ethics of that participation.

5 Organizational change as ensemble improvisation

- The enabling trap of professional practice
- Collective storytelling
- Enacting our sense-making
- Forum Theatre: showing us how we do what we do
- Ensemble improvisation – constructing the future together
- Agency in human affairs

The enabling trap of professional practice

For many, the word *practice* means 'a knowingful doing'. As a noun we can take it to imply a doing that is stabilized through repetition and so has come to mean an 'accepted knowingful doing' as in our sense of 'professional practice'. It is thus a way of working which is sustained and evolves in the interaction of a shifting community of people who are involved in various ways with this particular kind of doing. Like all such socially-constructed meanings, it is only partially specified by existing institutional forms and physical/technological constraints and always open to further specification. In the constant recounting and accounting to ourselves and one another of what we are about, we are persuasively making sense of our world of human action. The more professionalized an activity becomes, the more codified. A core of repetitively sustained, habitual ways of recounting and accounting are kept alive between increasingly clearly identified members of the profession. A systematic practice discourse of word and deed develops which increasingly comes to police the very terms in which the ongoing contesting of the practice is conducted. The great value of such professional discourses are that they allow us to argue retrospectively about what has happened and why, and to argue prospectively for what we should do for other things to happen and why. In this sense they legitimize the kind of causality we will use to articulate the nature of our human agency, the kind of difference we can make, the scope and limitation of our power to influence the evolution of events. As pointed out in the last chapter, professional discourses serve the ongoing constitution of different forms of social relations, in other words how we are to organize ourselves, and are always political.

Yet it is important to keep remembering that all such systematic discourses are a jointly sustained way of ordering the essentially vague and open nature of our communicative action in the living present. As I have already noted, within the rationale of an accepted systematic discourse, aspects of our experience become *rationally invisible* to us, the discourse itself does not afford us opportunities to draw attention in certain ways, and a certain kind of voice is literally unable to speak. This sense of being constrained in a prison one is helping to sustain can affect all of us.

Some years ago I remember joining a task force in a local authority called the Performance Management Action Team. A large part of their discussion was taken up with the design of overheads for presentation to the Executive Management Team. Their proposals centred on creating a number of different pilots to introduce the notion of performance appraisal as opportunities for dialogue rather than the production of the right paperwork. This felt to them quite a radical proposal. My colleague, Bill Critchley, and I pointed out how the conversation we were joining also seemed focused on the production of paper rather than the kind of dialogue they might want to have with members of the EMT. Could they leave aside the idea of the Task Force leader making a formal presentation to EMT, and instead imagine several members of the team engaging in a more open-ended dialogue about the issues raised by their work so far? It was interesting that one senior member of the group responded very strongly to stop this line of inquiry: 'They'll tear you apart!' he said, addressing the Task Force Leader. 'You'll look as though you have no idea what you're doing. Your career will suffer.' Despite this apocalyptic scenario my colleague and I continued to encourage discussion about the value and rationale for having such a conversation with the EMT. Slowly several members of the group began to make sense of this idea and to elaborate its possibilities. After a while it no longer seemed so outrageous and the Task Force leader became visibly enthused and was clearly imagining herself engaged with others in such a conversation. The meeting ended with a strong sense, despite some disquiet, that this was a way forward.

A few days later, the Task Force leader called me:

> Look, I know this might sound odd, but I would be very grateful if you would call into my office when you are next in the Borough. At the meeting I felt that I glimpsed something very important about how

to continue with our work in the Task Force and a whole ripple effect of possibilities that could flow from that. I felt really excited, but since then, as I've tried to talk with my colleagues that glimpse is disappearing. I just can't speak about it convincingly, I feel increasingly implausible and feeble the more I try. I want to talk with you again so that I can recreate what I was beginning to glimpse at that meeting and *be able to talk about it*!

This remains with me as a vivid example of the silencing of certain aspects of experience in certain dominant discourses and that certain 'traditions of argumentation' amplify or diminish our sense of self, the kind of person we feel we can be, the nature of our agency in the world. This senior manager reached out to me to amplify certain 'developing tendencies of feeling' that we recreated in our responsive communication with one another. In particular, we spoke in ways that began to legitimize a different kind of causality, a different way of accounting for how change has happened and could happen. We met several times to talk together about this and, as we did so, we both developed the personal resources to draw attention differently, to point to and sustain different possibilities in the conversational life of the Borough. We developed together a shift in the way we could speak of our organizational practice, hers as a manager, mine as a consultant. It was an increasing number of such experiences that began to give me a rather different way of talking about the kind of 'coaching' and 'facilitating' that I was interested in developing as an organizational practitioner. Instinctively I turned to talking and working with people with very different histories of professional practice, in particular those who had developed the craft of ensemble theatre work and storytelling and whose accounting for the nature of their agency had a different history from the one commonly sustained in organizations.

Collective storytelling

Some years ago I was invited to work with members of a network of Swedish managers, management educators, and consultants who were jointly engaged in developing the theory and practice of organizational change. Each year the network organized a few seminars to stimulate discussion. On this occasion I was to provide the stimulus, by introducing ideas about complexity and self-organizing emergence and the implications of this way of thinking.

I was acutely conscious of the expectations that I would introduce and develop a clear progression of ideas that would lead towards some kind of different model of organizational change whose implications for practice methodology we could identify, discuss and assess. Instead the evening before I was staring out of the window of my room, gripped in a silent rehearsal of my imagination in which I started this way or that, appealed to this or that experience, asked this or that question . . . No final organization of my thoughts into a sequence of topics would settle. I wanted to find a way to simultaneously describe, account for and illustrate a practice in a way that might bring it to life even in a seminar setting, a context rather different from that in which practice takes place day to day. Could I find a mode that matched the subject matter?

I was stimulated by two recent experiences. I had participated in a series of social dreaming sessions convened by Peter Tatham (1998) a practising Jungian analyst. He was working with participants at a conference, any of whom could join (or not) the sessions he convened for an hour before the rest of the proceedings each morning. Peter arranged the chairs in the room in which we gathered in a haphazard way so that no particular pattern could be easily discerned and we were all facing in many different directions. This arrangement created a sense of a web or network rather than the group evoked by a circle of chairs. He then invited us to tell any dreams or fragments of dreams we were having at or before the conference. People were asked to respond to what they heard not by any interpretation or analysis but by making links to their own dreams or to any image or association that arose. Peter participated by offering sometimes his own dreams/associations and by linking creatively to the themes of the conference, something we were all invited to do. We stopped after an hour and simply repeated this the next day with whoever had gathered again. Peter has his own way of thinking about the process at work, drawing on Jungian thought. I was enormously tickled by this experience in relation to my evolving practice. For me it was an extraordinary way of commenting on and working with the multiple experiences of the conference that answered the question, 'What are we talking about here?' in a way that wove us imaginatively into the social history of our gathering. As long as we stayed patiently with the sometimes stuttering flow of contribution, accepted to be sometimes bored and drifting, we were rewarded with unexpected insight reverberating differently amongst us, producing profound hilarity or intense stillness. The rich meanings we created between us were never fully articulated, always slightly beyond our grasp like the tail of a dream whisked out of sight as, waking, we try to catch it. Far from being inconsequential and ephemeral, those taking part in this activity agreed that it greatly affected their participation in the conference.

The second experience was that of an international storytelling festival in Forest Row, near where I live. Ashley Ramsden and his colleagues have developed a school for encouraging and evolving the ancient craft of oral storytelling. They introduced an activity to show us all our innate narrative skill. In pairs one person began telling a story, while their partner threw them words from time to time that must be incorporated into the evolving tale. This person was encouraged to offer words to throw the narrator off track. Who was more challenged, the narrator or the interrupter? The mutuality of the teller and the told, even one who was ostensibly derailing the telling was revealing. As we warmed to our task we both surprised ourselves and each other by the reciprocal creativity of our associations.

Back in Sweden, these experiences were influencing the way I approached the seminar. After some introductory remarks on the themes of self-organizing emergence, I asked people to arrange their chairs in a haphazard way, facing different directions. I started by asking everyone to join me in playing a simple game of word association. Someone was to start by saying a word and the 'next' person would say another word associated with the preceding one. The question of next was ambiguous, as it was not immediately obvious who was next in the haphazard arrangement of chairs. The sequence of people speaking was always a little uncertain and did not automatically repeat itself. Sometimes people spoke simultaneously. Some did not speak at all. This process ran for a while and then we talked together about what had struck us, what sort of patterns we discerned and how we made sense of the experience, and, in particular, *how our sense-making evolved as we continued to talk together*.

I will describe the evolution of this conversation without trying to ascribe remarks to different individuals. My intention is not to recapture an exchange word for word, but to illustrate something of the movement of meaning as it is constructed amongst a group of people relating to each other, and experienced by one member. I am not suggesting that what follows is a unified single thread of meaning that emerged for all. We remained sitting in a messy chair arrangement and the conversation developed haphazardly as different contributions elicited further responses – I was not managing the conversation, although of course I had convened it – a whole variety of different threads of meaning are likely to have been created.

The conversation went something like this.

Someone commented that the associations would run for a while in a way that felt unsurprising. Although no one could predict what the next person would say, when the word came it seemed to fall recognizably into place. Someone else mused that it seemed as though an unspoken idea or theme we might all share was inviting the associations. For example when the sequence went 'roof', 'floor', 'walls', 'picture', 'nail', 'hammer', someone said that it was as if a more or less shared image of 'house' then 'home' was suggesting these associations. Probably better to put it the other way round, another person suggested. Could we say that the relationships between words in the evolving series created this unarticulated, but largely shared glimpse of an emerging scene? I commented that we seemed to need to explain the common sense of pattern either by an idea sitting *behind* our associations, as it were, propelling them forward, or else an idea *in front of* them, drawing them forth. Was there any other way to think about this? Of course, someone else said, this 'organizing idea or theme' did not actually exist anywhere. No one had actually thought this at the time, had they? We had just created this notion as a useful tool for thinking together.

The suggestion was made that we could think of the posited 'organizing idea' as itself subtly shifting and evolving as we went along. However, the next remembered contribution, 'head', was perceived as a switch to a different pattern, rather than an evolution of the same pattern. Others agreed. Did anyone actually think this way during the game? No one had, we were making fresh sense together now. We were trying to account to ourselves for the consensus in hindsight about a switch in pattern, about sameness and difference.

Likewise it was noticed that certain of these imagined organizing scenes or ideas returned from time to time seeming to 'draw' a sequence back into a pattern already visited. We noticed how we gave agency to our notion of an organizing idea, then took it back – after all, each of us kept making a choice, the agency lay with each of us, didn't it? Often these 'returns' to a pattern we recognized did not repeat the same sequence as before, maybe only one word was actually repeated, but the sequence was generally agreed to be of the same 'family'. What happened when someone uttered a very surprising association? This 'broke' the pattern, people remembered feeling that something seemed to collapse, disintegrate, before another pattern got going. However, the collapse was not total; people pointed out that there was always a seed of a new pattern forming as the previous one dissolved. Again it was bafflingly difficult to locate this seed, it was not 'in' either word, nor between two words, but seemed to be a potential emerging after several words that we recognized as we looked back. So our sense of pattern was dynamic, had a fragile stability, sometimes very short-lived, sometimes lasting longer, but at the same time each pattern was also evolving and could unpredictably transform.

This discussion about the word-association game produced an atmosphere in the room that I experienced as an anticipatory alertness, in which I fancied people were intrigued by the conversation they had just participated in rather than the game itself. I suggested we try a development of this activity. The chairs were moved around to disturb any existing pattern that had been created in the way certain people followed one another. This time I asked the person who started to say a sentence or phrase. Whoever followed was to say another sentence or phrase that began to tell a story. We would keep going until we ran out of steam or agreed to stop or the story came to an end. As before, we talked about this experience, first in small groups and then all together.

Someone said that this was even more interesting than the first activity because what each person said had to make emerging sense of much that had gone before. I asked what 'emerging' meant. 'Emerging sense' carried with it the idea of something evolving, in the process of becoming more itself although it sometimes became something else. There was laughter at this, a kind of appreciation for the sense of seeming nonsense? Several people noted another paradox as each came to speak his or her contributing phrase: in a way you could say what you liked, no one could predict what you would say, but people agreed that you couldn't say *anything*. Our evolving story moved out of a history into an open-ended future, as though it created its own constraints and possibilities, that you could appreciate as it evolved but could not explain or predict in advance. The story evoked possible contributions and each contribution developed the story. Who or what was in charge of the story's change and evolution? All of us! None of us in particular! The story itself! No answer was entirely satisfying. We felt that we knew more about the nature of this experience than we could adequately say.

How had people experienced the act of contributing to the story? A number of people said that they had felt a surprising degree of inner tension as the moment came when they felt themselves to be 'next'. For some this tension had become paralysing, their minds had gone blank, they had to force something out, or let the moment pass. Others tried to prepare themselves by rehearsing possible next sentences as each one was uttered. Others found the sentences framed themselves in the speaking, they had an intuitive flash about how to continue but they heard their own words as they emerged from their mouths.

Had anyone tried to develop an intention to take the story in a particular direction? Some had. Was this successful? Yes and no. Perhaps for a few contributions, then the story veered off in ways not envisaged. Many people remembered the moment when one person had offered a sentence that re-framed the story so far as having taken place on a television programme being watched by a new set of characters, creating the sense of a drama within a drama. Had the person nursed that intention? Yes, he had realized the possibility of doing this and looked for an opportunity. He had had a sense of seizing the right moment to make his contribution. People realized that this shift of context could be repeated again and again leading potentially to an infinite regress of worlds within worlds and was in some way a device to create novelty which would itself become stale and irritating.

There were other moments when someone's contribution was surprising in a way that 'fell flat'. 'It just didn't connect enough.' 'Everything disintegrated.' 'The sense was lost.' 'It all unravelled.' 'I felt annoyed. I wanted to blame Lars for destroying the whole thing, yet that didn't seem quite fair as in another way I felt that we just couldn't keep the story moving.'

Could we ascribe leadership in shaping the story we constructed together? It was possible to identify, in retrospect, key moments when the story took creative leaps, but at the time each moment in the movement of the story was experienced as a moment full of uncertainty and potential. What was more, sometimes what we decided were key moments turned out to be based in misunderstanding or mistaken hearing of what someone thought they had said. Yes, what Eric had said, what Piers had said, now seemed particularly significant in different ways but only because of what had been said next and next and next. It was as though an unspoken potential in their contributions had been amplified in subsequent contributions. But this potential was not 'there' waiting, it was only created in further speaking. The story eluded all attempts to make causal attributions to any individual, yet we all felt accountable. If you had said that instead of that . . . but of course we can't know what might have happened!

Was this whole experience taking place at a purely verbal level? We could have taped the activity and then we would have had the story as a product that could be listened to again. A woman said that the experience was much more than that. The story-in-words, she said, was the tip of the iceberg. The experience was as much about the unspoken as about what was actually said. 'I am sure we were affected by our relationships with each other, by our smallest movements, by noises and shifts of light in and beyond this room and by memories and feelings triggered for each of us.' Even if we had videotaped the activity we could not have 'captured' all of this. She had felt wholly engaged during the activity with quite a range of thoughts and feelings. Others agreed. Just think, she said, how often we could do this, starting again with one person's phrase, even the same person and the same phrase, and we would probably never repeat ourselves. 'I feel as though the unspoken context between us is seething with possible stories we could bring into existence.' 'Including this conversation,' someone said. 'This conversation is another storytelling, our attempt to make sense of our previous storytelling. And it never stops, does it?' Sounds in the room of what – amusement? despair? delight? boredom?

How did people judge the quality of the story that had emerged? How well had we 'performed'? Immediately this evoked conversation about how creative the story was or was not. Did it come alive? Some people said that it went 'dead' in parts, became mechanical, stuck in a groove, for example when the phrase 'and then the duck quacked' kept returning. At first this had been funny and spontaneous, but then was experienced by several as frustrating and some admitted that it became a device, an easy way of dealing with the moment of creative tension, a collapse to a habit. A good quality story, someone said, was like a life story. A good story developed as if it had a life of its own. We fabricated a story that did not follow a predetermined script nor became a random load of nonsense. We created novelty and coherence, developed form and structure, contributed to collapse and destruction. We participated in the creation of form together, yet the form could evolve and surprise us. The story came to matter to each of us and clearly our contributions mattered to the story, could make a difference to it and yet not in ways we could control. We could each develop intentions, stratagems and aspirations about the story, yet could only act and influence in the opportunity of the present moment as we related to each other's contributions. It was all very engaging, frustrating, hopeful, alarming, funny and sometimes boring.

'What had our participation in the morning's conversational storytelling got to do with our understanding of the way organizations are sustained and changed?' I asked. There was a rather long pause in the room. Eventually someone laughed and said, 'Everything! It has everything to do with it, but I don't know how to put it!' We took a break that lasted the best part of an hour due to the animated conversations that developed around the coffee bar.

My intention in starting the seminar in this way was to evoke the experience of collective storytelling as an example of self-organizing sense-making. We were all able to keep drawing on this experience as I continued to try to articulate what the participant I quote above found so difficult to say. The overt task was to co-create a single narrative, the Story, one contribution at a time, which had a start, a development and came to an end. The creation of the Story was an example of communicative action, people literally had to relate to one another's contributions to produce something together. I asked people how they would propose to lead, manage or change the storytelling process? Clearly I could have given lots of constraints within which people were to work. The storytelling must take only so long, it must produce a Story about elephants which must be set in China. The Story must end well and words that begin with a B are disallowed. What fascinated people was that however many constraints and instructions I gave, whatever strategies I and others used to influence the Storytelling as it continued, there remained an essential unpredictability to the particular Story that emerged and an essential complexity in the dynamic that produces it.

However it was not just the Story itself that I wanted to draw people's attention to. I hoped people on the seminar might notice something of their experience of participating in the self-organizing process of meaning-making. I wanted to help them notice this not just in hindsight in relation to their creation of 'the Story' but as they continued to engage each other in a conversation that was making sense of the activity, telling further stories, with a small 's'. I mean by this that they were engaging in multiple narratives of remembering what had happened, putting their experience together in new ways and imaginatively and playfully speculating and proposing ways of making sense of it. This is also what I mean by communicative action. I know from later comments that, for some at least, this process caught up with itself and became a heightened reflexivity in the present – generating the kind of insight that it is very difficult to immediately summarize or pin down, in part because it is so paradoxical.

Emboldened by this experiment I continued to make connections with practitioners in the arts and drama, wanting to bring what I felt was a fertile collaboration more directly to my consulting work.

Enacting our sense-making

I arranged to have coffee one day at the Barbican with Piers Ibbotson, who was responsible for persuading the RSC to set up a small group called Directing Creativity to work with organizations. We met to explore our interest in complexity and self-organization and the way these ideas spoke to our practice. Piers was finding that companies were asking him to run workshops for managers to teach them theatre skills and to give talks on the art of theatre direction. I asked him if he was interested in working more directly with managing *as* a performing art, not by teaching transferable skills but by joining managers in the conduct of their work. He was eager to do this but said it was difficult to find such opportunities.

Not long after this I was talking with a business unit leader in an organization I was working with. She was recently appointed in a difficult situation in which the entire *raison d'être* of her business area was in flux and she felt that she needed to take a very different approach with her team of managers to navigate their way through this period of uncertainty. She wanted my help with a proposed 'strategic meeting'. I told her about my discussion with Piers and his analogy of the rehearsal room for a management meeting. What did she think of creating a space for a group of 'organizational actors' to develop together as an ensemble their ability to work with the 'materials' of their situation – evolving roles and script as scenes in a larger evolving drama? We also talked a little about Shotter's analogy of the manager as 'practical author.' These analogies spoke to aspects of her circumstances that this business leader was most concerned about and she was bold enough to decide to try the experiment. We decided not to over-prepare for this and, rather, to approach the proposed meeting as an interdisciplinary gathering of practitioners – managers, organizational consultant and theatre director – bringing their different professional backgrounds to the imminent discussion about the business.

This decision seems to me in retrospect to have been crucial to the success of the experiment. By gathering without spending a great deal of effort trying to pre-assign the nature of our contributions or how best to use our different experience or how to structure our time well, we placed ourselves in a situation where we were all acting (in the everyday sense) into the unknown. We were more than usually alert to the need to weave our actions in with one another to construct together an exploration that would be of practical value. The team leader began in narrative mode as I have already described in previous chapters, making sense of the moment by relating strands of previous discussion, decisions, events and to create a persuasive rationale for the present circumstances. I encouraged a free flow of conversation in response to her contribution and, as this gathered momentum, Piers listened carefully. Inevitably the exploration brought in 'a cast' much larger than those gathered in the room. He began to ask whether people could show him rather than just tell him about the complexities they were experiencing. At first we found it difficult to know what this might mean, but with his prompting and suggestions we got to the point of pushing back the furniture and using the space created for enacting various fragments of the larger drama this business unit was a part of. We moved from making visible the alliances and tensions amongst the team, to discussion with members of the company's executive, to scenes with staff at a regional centre, to negotiations with other business sectors, to dealing with the concerns of customers. People volunteered to represent the voice and stance of other individuals and groups. Piers encouraged people to be less reliant on speech alone to express themselves and soon people were using their bodies more, using the space itself, crude props and visual metaphor. There were times that the scenes flowed, there were moments of tension, hiatus, frustration and loss of inspiration. Sometimes the scenes would develop in ways that struck chords in the group and we would return to these, replaying variations to discover how things evolved differently with small variations at crucial moments.

This process continued until about four in the afternoon when a thoughtful, quieter mood seemed to emerge. Piers left at this point and I suggested that people take a break and talk in twos and threes about the significant themes of the day and the agenda of work. This gave rise to the next day's discussions. When people reconvened, one group proposed their agenda and the others added and amended in the light of their own conversations. A number of topics and decision areas were rapidly agreed and next day the group worked through these steadily in a relaxed manner. As we mulled over the experience of the whole meeting, one of the managers noted that this was the first time after a significant business meeting he was going home for the weekend feeling refreshed and in good spirits rather than exhausted. Another commented that, although he was often involved in 'strategic meetings', this was the first time the experience had lived up to his aspirations for that label. He felt he had been called on to contribute the widest range of his intelligence and knowledge about what was going on in the business. Another commented that the enactments had given him a greater appreciation of what his colleagues thought and felt on many issues and indeed, he laughed, he felt much clearer about his own position on a number of points. Piers told me later that this had been one of the most satisfying instances of organizational work he had been involved with. Over the next nine months, I joined the team regularly as this business area was entirely reconfigured and this earlier meeting continued to bear fruit.

The experience of this meeting left me thoughtful about the nature of spontaneity. I recalled many occasions as both a manager and a consultant when I had attended workshops, teambuilding events or management development courses where I had experienced some aspects of the way we worked together at this meeting. Role plays, line ups, group sculpts, biography work and so on were used as learning exercises. In each case the workshop leader or facilitator would introduce the activity, explain its purpose and instruct us in how to undertake it, debriefing afterwards to assimilate the learning. This meeting did not resemble that situation at all. Although we were all drawing on our experience in different ways, we did not set up our activities in advance of engaging in them, we moved into them, exploring and creating them together and learning in them as we went along. The analogy of a rehearsal room was only partly valid in so far as other people would in the future be responding to the implications of the understanding and potentialities we were 'playing with', not as 'audience' but as co-actors in the 'drama'. And the exploration was 'live performance' to ourselves; what we said and did altered the living reality of relationships and interdependencies of people in the room and beyond. I felt that the experience of the meeting had not shown me a new 'technique', rather it had taken further my interest in the self-organizing emergence of conversing. In surroundings and contexts where they feel less restrained, people in conversation are often animated, will gesture freely, will mimic or exaggerate as they bring in remembered or imagined others. It was Piers who introduced the phrase *ensemble improvisation* to talk about what we were doing, and it gave me a sense of the range of conversational life in organizations from the highly-staged set pieces to this ongoing improvisational mode.

Forum Theatre: showing us how we do what we do

Some years before this meeting I was involved with another project that used a theatrical approach to organizational issues. This was the London Borough I have already mentioned at the start of this chapter. It was moving into the era of public–private partnerships and a demand for more entrepreneurial, less bureaucratic approaches to running a wide range of services. Our remit was to help foster the 'cultural changes' the CEO felt were necessary to reorientate the Borough's approach to its responsibilities, although as ever the precise nature of these changes was far from clear. A major organizational change initiative was underway. A number of task forces had been set up. One of these was an Employee Communications Task Force which was struggling with a conflict of views about their brief. This was rooted in very different understandings about the nature of communication itself.

Some members saw communications in terms of behavioural rules governing the effective transmission of clear 'messages' and that the focus of the task force was to recommend improvements of a technical nature – the telephone system, IT links, bulletins, briefing chains and so on. They wanted to research best practice, draft policy statements on communication and write recommendations for managerial behaviour. Other members of the group saw the issues of poor communication as exactly to do with this emphasis on communication as unproblematic message transmission rather than meaning-making, but were having difficulty thinking about how to communicate this in their recommendations to the Executive Management Team. They came up with the idea of asking the Drama Centre, which produced theatrical events for the Borough's schools, to illustrate some communication vignettes at a meeting with the Executive Management Team in order to show what they meant and to stimulate discussion. In subsequent conversations with myself and my colleague, and with members of the Drama Centre, the idea began to grow. Why not produce something that more people would see? Why not produce a play about the Borough? Why not get the organization to produce the material for such a play?

A theatre director and scriptwriter from the Drama Centre began talking to people about the idea. We suggested that the next Forum could be used to generate material. The Forum was a regular meeting open to all staff of the Borough that we had initiated as an opportunity for exploration of how the Borough was changing. At this event, which the mayor happened to attend, a circus of chairs was created and the Director explained how he was going to work. Three professional actors began just two or three exchanges in a scene set in the Borough. Three small groups of five people volunteered to work with each character. At any time any group could call time out and each group went into a huddle with their character for one minute to suggest how the character might be responding to the evolving situation. The starting exchanges involved someone questioning the wording in the minutes circulated to staff after a management meeting. We suggested that the other people present also form small groups to discuss how things should develop. In this way, out of a mess of constant interruption, reassessment and further improvised exchanges a surprisingly coherent mini-drama began to emerge which caught the imagination of all those present and led to very animated discussion. Only later did I recognize that this idea of Forum Theatre had an important political history in the work of Augusto Boal, dramatist, theatre director and political activist. As a Member of Parliament in Rio de Janeiro in the mid-1990s Boal used street forum theatre to explore the situated conflictual complexities that people experienced trying to live their lives in the city and used the patterns that emerged as a basis for bringing forward new legislative proposals (Boal, 1998).

The theatre activity at the Borough was so successful that a paragraph was put in the Borough staff newsletter inviting more people to take part in further such sessions. Within two months the scriptwriter had used the material generated to create a play lasting an hour and a half. The interest of the mayor and the CEO helped to get a small amount of funding to produce the play. In collaboration with the Employee Task Force, the Drama Centre mounted the play for members of the organization. This was very well produced and acted, provocative and funny in parts, with many themes being explored on stage simultaneously, and with a highly ambiguous ending. It traced the attempt of a new manager in a fictitious organization to introduce change in the way her department worked. Did the organization change or not? The play was understood in many different ways by its audiences. It was given twenty performances, morning and afternoon for two weeks in May 1996, with anyone in the organization being invited to book a seat for a performance. Just under a thousand people saw the play.

Members of the Communications team, the director and actors engaged the audience in discussion about the issues raised afterwards and continued to elaborate with them the way the action could develop. Members of other organizations in the Borough and people from other boroughs in the city were invited to a special evening performance. The play was so well received that performances were commissioned by other organizations, the fees thus earned offsetting the costs of the production.

We discussed with the Communications group how they might work further with the energy and debate that the drama had stimulated. A letter was sent to everyone who had attended the play, encouraging them to continue the discussion within their working units. In order to help stimulate this, a group of twenty 'facilitators' volunteered to be available to groups who felt they needed help in getting such a discussion started. We helped this group discuss how they might approach such conversations. The aftermath of the performances continued to ripple through parts of the organization for several months and several further performances were mounted at the request of particular groups. From a small beginning, a rather unusual form of employee and management development had been created around the themes of change and communication. The cycle of the drama's creation, performance and assimilation arose in a self-organizing way as we all acted into the opportunities that emerged. As with any novel development, this took shape amid differences and conflicting intentions, opportunities made and actions taken whose outcomes could not be known. People formed alliances, persuaded, gained influence, found resources as they went along. There was design and planning, but not of an overarching kind that had a complete 'vision' of a project in mind in the early stages. In contrast, extensive designs and proposals were being prepared in the management and staff education department on exactly these themes. These proposals took nearly a year to be actioned and created much less impact.

Ensemble improvisation – constructing the future together

This led me to get to know a Danish company, DaCapo Teatre, who had been using Forum Theatre in organizations for some years. The head of the company invited me to Denmark to join fifty managers, consultants, academics and actors to a conference with Keith Johnstone, who has spent a lifetime working with improvisation in the theatre, since his days at the Royal Court in London in the 1950s. Each day Keith worked with us to develop wonderfully bizarre, comic and moving scenes in hundreds of brief improvisations involving a handful of us at any one time. We all had the repeated experience of participating as actors and audience in these live performances. My contribution at this conference was to make sense of organizational change in ways that would resonate with the work that Keith was doing with us. Although the kind of improvisation that Keith was introducing was far removed from the business settings in which I usually found myself, I felt again a thrill of recognition that stirred me to experience my own practice afresh. Keith did not use the concept of self-organization. Yet, to me, he lived and breathed a profound appreciation of the complex movement pointed to by this concept in the way he approached everything.

Keith Johnstone was involved with us in a particular kind of teaching and learning that was quintessentially paradoxical. From the start he introduced a conversational style, meandering, playful, associative, exploratory and responsive. He would shamble into the room, sit down with us and just start talking as though we were all in the middle of overt rather than silent conversation already. Unlike most presentational talk when one person talks to many, there was no sense of rehearsal, no following a sequence or plan, it was teaching that played around with certain themes entirely in keeping with its subject matter. The meandering way Keith talked was acutely sensitive to the silent responses of all the persons gathered there with him. It was as though he was immersed in the ebb and flow of anticipation, nervousness, curiosity, embarrassment, desire, interest, that each person was responsively contributing to the group conversation in which one person, Keith, was actually speaking. His talk flowed between bits of history, anecdotes, aphorisms, tips and speculations. He talked aloud about the responses he imagined we might have to what he was saying. He gave many variations of the paradoxical injunction so familiar for all creative endeavours: Don't *try*, don't try to be clever, don't try to be funny, don't try to please me, don't try to be good, don't try to get this right, that's sure to mess things up. Just respond spontaneously to what is happening. He teased us and made fun of himself, he was personal and authoritative by demonstrating how to be at ease with the situation evolving between us. His tone was quiet and conversational. It was, for me, as though we were all working out together how to begin, not to answer this question but to find ourselves beginning. And sure enough Keith sensed the moment to say casually, OK let us have four or five of you in the space here, and suddenly five people were getting out of their seats while the rest settled back dealing variously with mixed feelings of disappointment and relief.

Keith would offer the briefest sketch of a starting point, a situation, an initial gesture, nothing extraordinary. 'You have arrived at the door of a flat. It belongs to this person.' 'You are on a country lane. You are looking for a place to stop and picnic.' Each time we took it from there. It was not only the group of improvisers active each time, the audience responded moment by moment to the evolving improvisation just as the improvisers were responding to one another and to the audience. I was as aware of my bodily response as I watched as when I was improvising. We all made the scenes 'work' or not, we lent them more or less life, we glimpsed their possibilities or withdrew from them in discomfort. Whatever happened, Keith continued to muse and comment, provoke and attract another group of us into another and yet another scene. All the time he was drawing our attention this way and that, tickling our appreciation of the processes at work between us and so 'teaching' us this art from within our experience of doing it. He elaborated certain themes repeatedly.

The obviousness of originality

We experienced for ourselves over and over again that people's attempts to think up something original, slightly ahead of the developing action, actually produced the commonplace and often congealed the movement of the scene. The most novel and satisfying developments occurred as people allowed themselves to make in the act of gesturing, an unpredictable response that was recognizable and 'fitting' as it came because of the way the shape of whatever was happening could evolve. We experienced repeatedly the paradoxical obviousness of the unexpected next step. He points out in his book, *Impro* (Johnstone, 1979), that trying to be original is like trying to walk North from the North Pole, it can only take you further away from what would be an inevitably unique response in the first place.

Spontaneity

Keith would notice when an improviser paused, caught in a silent
conversation, and attempt to catch whatever they were in the process of
rejecting. Sometimes if he asked quickly enough the person would say
something and Keith would say lightly, 'No, just before that' and the
person might suddenly offer a word or phrase which in one way was
ordinary yet would immediately stir something amongst the rest of us.
Often such contributions at the moment of the paused improvisation
seemed to strike multiple *entendres*. This stirring in the audience of the
rejected next contribution was spontaneous – we were tickled before we
could precisely say why. And then immediately we would start making
the links and associations, often sexual, irreverent, clever, always
apposite at the precise moment. We resonated in various ways with the
improviser's discomfort – we all felt the pull towards and away from the
revealing nature of our spontaneous responses, we felt exposed in our
knowingness as the webs of associations rippled amongst us.

Keith made it clear that he was not interested in this phenomenon from a
Freudian interpretation of repressed contents of the unconscious
individual mind. He was showing us how, as we communicated with
ourselves and with one another, we were constrained by our history of
relating as social persons. If we did not interrupt the emergence of the
next and the next and the next response as they arose in us we delighted
and disturbed ourselves in a way we could scarcely bear. Like someone
always off balance and continuing to stay upright only by moving, the
ensemble evolved. To stop was to fall. As we gestured to one another in
the openness of the present engagement, the next spontaneous
contribution paradoxically created continuity with the past and
transformed its nature by opening a way forward which only became
recognizable as it was taken up by the next response. And this creativity
was of a very ordinary kind. Blood flowing with a mixture of pleasure
and embarrassment, alarm and satisfaction, as we all discovered that our
joint action was indeed beyond our individual control. As Keith pointed
out, in 'normal' life we create conditions together which keep our sense
of who we are and what kind of situation we are in much more stable and
repetitive. Such conditions include the technologies, ideologies and
institutional forms that we sustain together. In the imaginative world of
improvisation, and with Keith's deft encouragement, the constraints
became our capacity to accept and move with whatever was happening. It
is hard to bear such a degree of rapid evolution, either socially,

organizationally or personally, such fluidity of individual and group identity. Yet the experience was very instructive. It made it hard to hold on to the humanistic notion of an essential, authentic unitary self as an inner possession of our subjectivity.

The relational nature of drama

Keith gave four people simple role descriptions as individuals and asked them to improvise a scene of arriving at the house of one of them. What would happen next? The result was rather stiff and dull. Then he asked the same people to choose some aspect of their relation to each of the other persons, such as 'I admire you' or 'you irritate me' or 'I'm in awe of your reputation'. The result was a transformation, the scene flowed with ease and seemed full of subtlety and inventiveness, a pleasure for the audience and 'actors' alike. He mused that sterile improvisation invented characters and asked them to interact, whereas life-like theatre invented complex relations and showed how scenes, plots and characters evolved together.

How responsiveness creates evolution

Rather than trying to take the initiative, Keith Johnstone showed how responsiveness was key. Only if people concentrated on responding to whatever others offered, so as to continue to make sense of what had happened and what might happen, could the ensemble sustain itself. Like the paradoxical nature of originality, this stimulated much discussion about the way we usually understand leadership and initiative by ignoring the patterning of responses from which something later recognized as an act of leadership emerges. The paradox here was that of freedom and constraint, that individual creativity made no sense except as a social phenomenon.

The inescapable creation of power difference in human relating

Keith encouraged us to play what he called 'status games' and showed us how, in the tiniest of gestures and shifts of tone or body position, this was always at work. There was no such thing as a level playing field. He made this quite graphic by inviting us to enact many 'master–slave scenes' in which the exquisite dance required to sustain the relationship was very apparent. It was difficult for both parties. Above all he showed that the greatest interest and novelty was created when very small variations in power difference between a number of people were at work. He made it impossible not to face up to the ubiquity of this aspect of relating, and its paradoxical nature; that all relating was simultaneously enabling and constraining.

As the conference progressed, I was stuck by how I was being shown very vividly much about the nature of complex responsive processes of relating that my colleagues and I were attempting to articulate more conceptually. Similarly I was able to articulate what members of DaCapo were doing in ways that offered a new rationale for their work. All of us were excited by the way our practice evolved in these conversations.

Agency in human affairs

I am making a particular appeal to storytelling and theatre in this chapter. I am not suggesting that exposing people to these arts can improve their presentational and persuasive skills, although no doubt this is so. Rather, I am using storytelling, drama and ensemble improvisation in particular, as a way of bringing attention to the place of spontaneity in the emergent processes of communicative action. Of course, I am not saying that organizational change is only this improvisatory process where the constraints are our investment in our sense of self in a virtual world of the imagination. In organizations this is bolstered by heavy investment in the material and technological and institutional ramifications of social patterning. Nevertheless, the analogy highlights an essential aspect of the process of social and organizational change.

People working with the improvisational arts as a discipline are particularly alive to the paradoxical process of our intentional participation in the immediate processes of human relating. We each contribute to patterning communicative action that patterns further communicative action. These practitioners have an appreciation of human agency very different from the way this is largely conceived in organizations. There we tend to focus on leadership and influence in terms of our ability to articulate strategies, goals and desired outcomes which we impose on an imagined future as templates in the form of project plans. Our sense of our own agency is tied up with being able to account for ourselves in these terms, to show that we can realize prior intention in the face of all kinds of difficulty and to think in very sophisticated ways prior to action. Hence the heroic nature of most leadership mythologies in organizations. In contrast, practitioners in the arts have an acute sense of the paradox of being 'in charge but not in control' as we strive to play out creatively the evolution of our interdependent and conflicting responsibilities and aspirations, forming and being formed in the process.

The theatre director Peter Brook (1990) expresses this clearly in his book, *The Empty Space*:

> The director will see that . . . however much home-work he does, he cannot fully understand a play by himself. Whatever ideas he brings on the first day, must evolve continually, thanks to the process he is going through with the actors . . . In fact, the director who comes to the first rehearsal with his script prepared with the moves and business etc. noted down, is a real deadly theatre man.
>
> (1990: 119)

Describing his own first realization of this, as a young director experiencing the divergence between his prepared ideas and what was happening among the actors, he says:

> My heart sank and despite all my preparation, I felt quite lost. Was I to start again, drilling these actors so that they conformed to my notes? . . . It was a moment of panic. I think, looking back, that my whole future work hung in the balance. I stopped, and walked away from my book, in amongst the actors, and I have never looked at the written plan since. I recognised once and for all the presumption and folly of thinking that an inanimate model can stand for man.
>
> (ibid.: 120)

I started by pointing out how current professional discourses of managing, consulting or facilitating themselves can become hermeneutically closed, sealing our very experience of ourselves. What I have illustrated here is that, as local communication between practitioners with diverse experiences takes place in specific action contexts, mutual recognition and differentiation occurs creatively in the detailed interaction of conversing/working together, evolving existing practices and spawning new ones in a non-systematic way. It is this same process that is continuously giving rise to innovative evolution in all our social practices.

6 The legacy of organization development

- Narrative sense-making
- Metaphorical sense-making
- Logical sense-making
- Organizational Development and process consultation
- Process, participation and the reflective practitioner
- Process consultation
- Learning to learn
- The learning organization
- Group relations
- From 'hard' to 'soft' systems

I introduced this book by saying it was about practice. What do I mean by that? People often complain that some proposition is fine in theory but it's different in practice. Concepts of theory and practice are usually distinguished and related in this way in common parlance. 'Theory' is meant to map onto 'practice' and rarely does so to our full satisfaction. The best we can do with this way of thinking is to keep reminding ourselves that the map is not the territory. Karl Weick, in his book *Sense-making in Organisations* (1995), expresses something of this dissatisfaction:

> To edit continuity is to render the world less unique, more typical, more repetitive, more stable, more enduring. However the world of continuous flows has not thereby become any less unique or transient . . . Thus there remains a chronic disjunction between the discrete products of sense-making and the continuities they map. Sense-making that is better able to bridge this disjunction and retain some of this continuity is likely to feel more plausible, and possibly be more accurate.
>
> (p. 108)

Notice that Weick seems to be implying that the best we can do to retain a sense of continuous flow is to try to close the gaps that our sense-making creates. We make sense in terms of a completed product *of* our experience. That experience is here offered as a continuous flow of a rather mysterious, unknowable kind, and the sense we make of it must inevitably carve it up and edit it. Could we instead theorize differently, so that we don't create gaps to be bridged, but instead think in the flow of experience itself? Then transience and endurance, novelty and familiarity arise simultaneously and spontaneously as aspects of the open-ended, always incomplete movement of experience. We are not making sense *of* experience. Rather sense-making *is* part of the movement of our experiencing:

> . . . sitting by an open window, reading, aware of the play of air currents on my skin, suddenly a new scent assails me, sweet and pungent, evocative yet elusive. I slacken the grip on my book as my nostrils flare and tiny muscles tense with the desire to connect this smell. My mouth waters slightly. 'Cloves' forms as sound and word silently, images flickering. I feel the yearning feeling subside, I begin wondering whether I preferred the intense feeling of a second ago or this new slightly disappointing feeling of locating the connection. I feel a slightly hollow sensation in my diaphragm. I begin thinking about language. My hands catch the book slipping from my lap. Shall I go on reading or not? I call to a friend across the room, 'Can you smell the cloves?' She lifts her head, smiles, pauses. 'It reminds me of Indian spiced tea.' She starts to rise from her seat, 'I bought some once, I must have it somewhere,' opening and closing cupboards and shuffling packets. I move across the room towards her. 'Here,' opening the packet, both of us sniffing the dry leaves with hints of orange rind and yes the cloves, not quite the same scent. Is it stale? 'Let's try anyway' . . .

I am suggesting that we can think of experience itself as a flow of body rhythms, rhythms that shift as we sense, feel, associate, imagine, name, think, speak, move, intuit, speculate. If we start to think in this way, sense-making no longer acts upon an undifferentiated flow. Instead the flow of experience is that of continuously patterned (differentiated) rhythms of living bodies relating in a world of relationships. It is this kind of sense-making which has come to seem to me to be more plausible, more resonant, even if when explicitly formulated such theorizing requires us to think paradoxically.

What are the implications for the way we speak of practice? The word 'practice' as a concept is often used to refer to patterns of activity that can be mapped and grasped as wholes distinct from the persons acting in particular times and places. These particular times and places can also then be conceptualized as 'contexts' – historical, cultural, physical –

which can also be mapped and grasped as whole patterns. The persons acting are understood in a similar way, in terms of 'mindsets', that can be mapped as wholes of another kind, patterns of assumptions, beliefs and values. Then we can map the way these wholes interact with one another as a further whole. This process of mapping is understood as the essence of reflection on experience, while experience itself continues as an undifferentiated flow apart from the way we are conceptualizing about it. So it is commonplace to create concepts of roles and jobs, professions and practices, organizations and markets and economies, all of which we can map out as patterns of activity and interaction. This common parlance, then, is a way of thinking and it is using a particular kind of logic, where I am using the word 'logic' to mean a particular way of distinguishing and relating concepts.

As an alternative to this way of thinking I have been writing about working as an organizational consultant, as my experience of the stream of responses my own and others' actions are calling forth from myself and others. Speaking, imagining, remembering, moving, feeling, designing, persuading, making connections, using tools, developing strategies, analysing situations, forming narratives, taking action in relation to others – this is what I mean by 'the flow of my experience'. The patterning of this responsive gesturing continues to pattern further responsive gesturing as the flow of complex interdependencies which are being sustained and potentially changed as this self-organizing relating continues. Persons experiencing a unique patterning of self-hood emerge. Such differentiated persons, groupings, activities, societies and cultures are then conceptualized, not in structures to be mapped separately from this process, but arising as the patterning of our living experience as bodies relating to one another and to aspects of the world we actively recognize. This communicative patterning involves the experience of simultaneous possibility and constraint that is emerging as the process of relating continues, producing repetition, habit, the familiar, and, at the same time, variations which may transform the patterning at all scales of detail as it flows on. Continuity and change are emerging simultaneously because the relating is always the relating of difference, of bodies with different histories of relating. In this series this way of thinking has been referred to as 'complex responsive processes of relating' (Stacey, 2001).

Making sense of living in the world in this way *is* my ongoing practice; it is what I do. My practice is the patterning of my sense-making, which is my theorizing. In writing this, it becomes clear that I am using a logic that links concepts like theory and practice in a paradoxical way. At first this may seem irritating or unnecessarily confusing. At first I may seem to be saying that two ideas that we have gone to all this trouble to distinguish are being collapsed to the same thing. But I am not saying that, because the paradoxical logic I am using to theorize here is a temporal rather than a spatial logic. It is a logic that distinguishes and relates concepts as emerging in a continuous flow of present experience rather than placing them in relation to one another as though presented to our gaze as a conceptual map. Such maps may show dynamic patterns of interactions, process maps, but they remain whole patterns removed from the flow of present experience and so are essentially spatial. Different logics deal with time in different ways. The purpose of this and the next chapter is to try to show the nature and implications of that difference when working with organizational continuity and change.

Narrative sense-making

Throughout the preceding chapters I have been exploring how organizational continuity and change emerge over time. I have been describing scenes and episodes of my experience of the everyday ordinary drama of people relating to one another at work. My stories themselves don't seem paradoxical. That is because the logic of narrative is necessarily temporal. I create and connect events over time, and meaning emerges as I write or someone reads. The kind of logic I am using remains implicit in such storytelling. The paradoxical nature of that logic only becomes apparent when I make the connections and relations explicit, particularly those that impute any kind of explanation, any kind of causality. The paradoxical nature of narrative is that it makes sense of what we can draw on (the past) in such a way that shapes our experience of a meaningful present (now) which includes where the story can go from here (the future). At the very same time, the way the narrative is opening up the future acts back on how the past leads towards it, and so further shapes our present experience. Interpretations of the past are influencing expectations of the future which are influencing interpretations of the past in the interactive present. This is the paradoxical, iterative, non-linear movement of narrative sense-making. I have used narratives to convey the way I am making sense without always formulating this explicitly. I have used Shotter's phrase of stories as instructive accounts because, of course, different stories make sense differently and reading different kinds of stories that different practitioners may offer begins to convey something of different ways of practising.

Metaphorical sense-making

I do not use maps and mapping metaphors. I have used metaphors of theatre and drama, particularly ensemble improvisation, to evoke a way of experiencing organizational life, suggesting that we imagine ourselves as actor–director–producer–authors whose actions as they arise in response to one another are perpetually creating an evolving live theatre of interweaving narratives. Sets, characters, scenes and their significance for us are emerging together as shifting configurations of meaningful association and connection across space and time. The kind of theatre I have in mind is more akin to improvised street theatre than a formally staged performance at Covent Garden, although we may recognize set-pieces like the regular weddings in our favourite soaps. Although we may experience ourselves at times as audience to aspects of the drama, we are always players, active contributors to the action. What happens next is always constrained by what has happened before. Yet the drama is always in the process of being reshaped as the significance of what is now understood as previous scenes and acts is recast, as new entities emerge and others disappear, as new developments of theme, plot and character are glimpsed, as constraints shift to offer different opportunities. Again this is the paradoxical nature of the experience of the flow of present time as we reshape the past and co-construct movement into the future in the way that I keep drawing attention to. The dramas evolve in a self-organizing way as we participate together in this social theatre. I have emphasized the spontaneous, improvisatory nature of this process. The word 'improvise' is often used to convey notions of unrehearsed, unpremeditated, unintentional, unmotivated action, but by linking it to ensemble in 'ensemble improvisation' I am again trying to get at the inherent paradox. All of us, with our conflicting intentions, plans, hopes, fears and choices emerging, are literally acting our way into plays that we are spontaneously forming and which are forming us at the very same time. We make a difference and become different in a patterning process we can never control. Of course, this social theatre does not float free of a world that is more than human relating. The social theatre includes all the props of human devising we inherit, from our buildings, to our mobile phones, to our transport system, to our regulatory policies and laws. As we use these props in our current interaction, we continue to shift the way they both constrain and enable us, just as the wider world of interaction which is our evolving natural world profoundly influences and is influenced by what is happening, as we are becoming increasingly aware.

Again my choice of metaphor helps me to convey implicitly the kind of logic I am using to relate concepts and ideas. This theatrical metaphor allows me to draw attention to the fact that an improvised play is only being realized through the detailed interaction of the cast as the live action of the theatre. Our sense of 'the play', meaning, arises continuously as we experience the narrative patterning of that live action in a unique way whereby we realize ourselves as differentiated yet interdependent 'players'. By our live action we are self-organizing in shifting social figurations that we are actively transforming and being transformed by, day in, day out. The twists and turns of personal/family/organizational/social/economic life, the familiar reprise, the novel developments and reversals, are to be understood in the evolution of the shifting meanings of the responsive interplay of the emerging players. It is important to remember that these are player–director–producer–authors as I said before, and all of them are playing with variously ambitious and strategic notions of the scenes and narrative themes they may be constructing that make sense of their own parts. However, none of them is outside the evolving action, able to direct the overall drama that is emerging. The drama and its meanings are always incomplete.

Logical sense-making

I want to distinguish between two different kinds of logical theorizing, that is, two different ways of linking concepts and ideas to one another. One kind is the logic of paradox reflected in the narratives of previous chapters. For this purpose I have been using a theatrical metaphor as a descriptive and evocative way of theorizing. Let us now explicitly take concepts such as local/global or individual/social. A paradoxical logic posits a single explanatory process in which these concepts emerge simultaneously as aspects of one and the same patterning movement of experience, that of direct interaction. Another kind of logic is the logic of both/and thinking in which concepts such as individual/social are explained as complementarities which together form a unity or a whole. The two concepts are linked by placing them at different logical levels and having one emerge from the other. This logic resolves paradox by introducing spatial concepts of wholes or systems beyond the immediate temporal process of direct interaction. This kind of logic is the formalism of systems thinking and it is reflected in the spatial metaphors of maps and territories or of lenses through which we look at organizations (Morgan, 1986).

Earlier volumes in this series have explored in detail the differences and implications of these different ways of theorizing with their different logics. The first volume (Stacey, Griffin and Shaw, 2000) distinguished between different ways that self-organization is understood as a causal process and introduced the idea of 'transformative teleology' to describe a paradoxical movement into a future that is under perpetual construction by the movement itself. To do this, we drew on Mead's interpretation of Hegel's dialectic which requires a paradoxical understanding of time. This is quite different from the Kantian dialectic which combines a 'rational teleology' of human action motivated by chosen goals, with the 'formative teleology' of systems thinking where movement into the future is an unfolding of what has been enfolded already. Instead of the present being a point in a grand sweep of time from past to future, the present is opened up, revealing its own micro movement, which we called the 'living present'. In the second volume (Stacey, 2001), the concept of complex responsive processes of relating was further elaborated. Stacey takes the work of Mead and Elias, strands of complexity thinking and relational psychology, to offer a way of thinking in which mind, self, society, power figurations and ideologies arise between us as the detailed, local interaction of communicating bodies in the living present. Stacey points out that this way of theorizing draws attention to the circular iterative processes of gesture–response at all scales as analogous to fractal patterning – the same patterning process being conceptualized at whatever degree of detail. Individual and group are then aspects of communicative process, not different phenomenal levels. Organizing is conversational process and organizational change is shifts in the patterning of conversation. In a later volume (Griffin, 2001), the difference between an account of organization as what we have called 'participative self-organization' and one based on concepts of systemic self-organization is explored in depth. Griffin examines the implications for our understanding of ethics and leadership that these two ways of thinking support. Again reinterpreting Mead's thinking, he shows how conceptualizations that focus on wholes unfolding according to enfolded principles run the risk of reifying those wholes so that intention and purpose are imputed to the wholes themselves. Thus leadership and ethics become located in the evolving wholes as idealized 'cult' values to which we willingly agree to submit ourselves.

In the remainder of this chapter, I will look back at the heritage of organizational development, highlighting the logic, metaphors and narratives of change that shape this way of sense-making and so practising. What I am paying attention to is how practitioners account to themselves and others for how they work, what matters and why.

Organizational Development and process consultation

Activity that came to be known as Organization Development (OD) brought a particular kind of rational inquiry to the art of improving the processes of human communication and organization. Practitioners advocated a planned and sustained effort to apply behavioural science to the improvement of organizational processes, using reflexive, self-analytic methods. Their stance was one of rational constructivism. Existing organizational processes might be poorly designed or suffering from lack of design, or they might simply be no longer fit for current circumstances, or the way they might be working in reinforcing or undermining one another might be poorly understood. Subjecting such processes to joint examination (mapping of some kind) on an organization-wide scale was bound to lead to the specification and implementation of improvements. OD 'interventions' were thus activities for stimulating 'organizational learning' as collective understanding of and action to change human systems and processes at a particular 'level' of an organization. Teams, departments, businesses, organizations, communities, societies, could be approached as nested open systems, each in dynamic exchange with an environment consisting of other systems across the system boundary. A range of OD technologies became widespread: process consultation, survey feedback, teamwork inventories, inter-group dialogues. All these interventions proposed that the purpose of intensive collective reflection was to create understanding of what gives rise to certain systemic patterns which would then foster the ability to generate alternative processes, to achieve chosen outcomes, again in terms of the patterns of systems behaviour. The kind of reflexive, self-analytic methods being proposed here *always ask people to reflect on and change the underlying patterns that are causing observable system behaviour*. Here we get the split between experiencing and making sense of experience that I have explored above.

In this chapter I would like to examine how this legacy has shaped our understanding of learning processes. This, in turn, has led to influential notions of managing learning organizations and managing culture, which are clearly different from the kind of learning processes I have been describing so far in this book.

Process, participation and the reflective practitioner

First let us go back to the practice of OD as it evolved amongst its originators. It is clear from the authors of the first Addison Wesley OD series published in 1969 (Beckhard, Bennis, Blake and Mouton, Lawrence and Lorsch, Schein, Walton) that they took up Kurt Lewin's 'action research' method (1946). This itself arose in response to a questioning of the existing theory/practice divide in which the pursuit of generalized knowledge had become separated from its application. Lewin's idea was to develop a practical social science which would distinguish itself from 'normal' scientific inquiry into the natural world in two ways. First, it was to be concerned with a *science of practice* that would be useful, valid, descriptive of the world *and informative about how we might change it*. Second, it advocated *cooperative research* that engaged throughout those people who were actually concerned with or affected by the problems and goals of the research process itself. This approach, Lewin hoped, would heal the split between pure and applied research and the unease created by doing research 'on' people rather than 'with' them. This was a major change of conversation, and action research became the primary methodology of OD, with the term 'research process' being replaced with 'learning process'. Organization development meant the intentional design of *effective, goal-directed learning processes* for individuals and collectives. The words 'process' and 'participation' began, as we will see, to accrue certain meanings within this conversation.

OD practice was very much shaped by the way learning processes were conceived in terms of individual cognitive models. Four phases are distinguished in an iterative cycle of learning. Immediate experience is the basis for observation and reflection by each of those involved in the inquiry. These data are then shared and assimilated into a theory of how the world works (a map or model) and how to intervene in such a world, from which new implications for action can be deduced. These implications or hypotheses then serve as guides for acting to create new experiences for further observation and reflection and further changes to the theories and models. This constituted an approach to experience and action that brought together a positivist scientific orientation and the idea of circular feedback processes in cybernetic models of self-regulating and adaptive organisms and ecologies. We are asked to understand ourselves as repeatedly pausing in the present to learn from the patterns of the past and thus design patterns to better serve our ends in the future. This is a particular way of thinking about our self-consciousness as humans. It involves key conceptual separations – analytical/diagnostic observation *of* our ongoing participation *in* 'structured (i.e. repetitive) human processes' in order to design the patterning of future action. The way OD practitioners described their work created highly complicated edifices of thought, whatever the scale of the analysis.

Process consultation

Take Schein's (1988) account of process facilitation. How does he explain what he is doing and what managers can learn to do? He invites us to observe communication in terms of each individual in a group initiating or responding to messages from others at observable intervals of observable duration, some of which are verbal and some non-verbal. In addition he invites us to notice how some of us are sending and receiving straightforward messages while, at other times, we can infer that people are distorting messages to conceal themselves or they are making decisions to reveal what they have been hiding. We may also notice how some may be responding to messages others are not aware they are sending, or vice versa, and we may also notice that there may be 'emotional contagion' as several parties are sending and responding to messages they are not aware of sending or receiving. Also we may observe that everyone, including ourselves, is operating with perceptual filters that affect what messages they select to send and to receive. We may also observe that these perceptual filters may lock into one another, creating circular loops or self-fulfilling prophecies. Finally, we may also see how regularities or norms of interaction may have established themselves over time. These norms or 'rules' may be more or less conscious, enabling or constraining individual behaviour in ways that may have become outdated in usefulness for the group. Very complex webs of norms start to constitute a culture which may or may not be helpful to the group.

It is all this sophisticated 'data' of human interaction that Schein says the process consultant is trained to observe in his/herself and others and then to feedback in a judicious and timely fashion to participants. The facilitator invites their joint diagnosis and helps them to make the changes they want to make to improve their own effectiveness, by agreeing to reduce distortions, miscommunications and ambiguities as far as possible and to reconstruct some of the norms with which they are regulating their own behaviour. Schein warns that 'one of the reasons culture is so difficult to change is that when norms begin to support each other, one must change the whole set of norms instead of just the one or two that are getting in the way' (1988: 79). It is clear that what we are thinking of changing here is a highly complicated conceptual mapping of observed regularities of interaction. It is very noticeable that any idea of change as a spontaneous process emerging as persons relate to one another while pointing to these maps is never considered. What Schein is always emphasizing and wanting to harness is our individual human capacity for conscious rational choice exercised on behalf of some whole pattern of interaction to be achieved by changing the detail of local interaction.

In the previous chapter I described how the art of ensemble improvisation highlights the kind of responsive communication in which continuity and transformation evolve simultaneously and spontaneously. It is telling to see how differently Schein uses the idea of 'Human Exchange as Drama' (1987: 82). He sees individuals learning to play a variety of roles in a variety of different scenes in life and marvels that 'One of the most amazing human capacities is our ability to keep in our heads the multiple scripts that apply to the many human dramas we play out.' The human drama of process consultation, he insists, depends on the clients remaining as actors while the process consultant remains in the role of audience, refusing to 'take the stage'. While keeping certain general principles in mind, the process consultant or facilitative leader must be innovative; 'they must vary their own behaviour according to the stream of feedback signals they get from their clients and must be prepared to rewrite their scripts constantly.' Schein refers to this as spontaneity and improvisation. A good practitioner can recognize 'scenes' and is able to flexibly rewrite his or her own scripts. This is very different from the way I have been using the terms 'spontaneity' and 'improvisation' to imply a paradoxical process of constructing an open-ended future that is constructing us at the same time.

Schein refers to his ways of making sense of human processes as *simplifying* models that allow us to grasp complex phenomena as dynamic wholes that act as practical guides to effective intervention in human systems. Let us look carefully at what is happening to the words 'process' and 'participation'. Process becomes a repetitive dynamic that can be isolated and observed. The aim of collective learning processes is to use one such dynamic to reach working agreements on diagnosis, goals for change and joint action to achieve them. These learning processes themselves can be observed and changed. The 'task' is something that can be conceptually distinguished from the 'process' , meaning the 'what' can be distinguished from the 'how' and even from the 'who':

> We can construct a picture of the group in terms of the actual members and their relationships to one another and to the task. The focus [could] be on the relationships among the members of the group, regardless of what the group is actually working on . . . just as it is possible to observe a group at work and abstract the methods it uses to accomplish that work, so it is possible to abstract the interpersonal processes evident in a group independent of the actual people involved in these processes.
>
> (Schein, 1987: 45)

Some processes become repetitive and stable as 'structured processes' and so can be conceptually distinguished from 'fleeting or transient processes'. 'Culture' becomes a complex of structured processes. This thinking is very much alive and well in organizations where managers repeatedly sponsor endeavours to 'map' processes at an intrapsychic, group, intergroup, organizational and societal level which will allow us to develop plans to 're-engineer' such processes. Participation begins to mean the involvement of those interacting in a given systemic pattern and a participative approach advocates identification and involvement of key 'stakeholders' in the process of learning and change in such an identified system.

Schein often emphasizes that the conceptual distinctions he makes 'in theory' are not so clear cut 'in practice' but he insists that *these distinctions are essential for making sense of experience and for guiding action*. I am dwelling on these points because, in this book, I am arguing that this kind of conceptualizing is *not* essential. It is only essential if creating maps as guides to action is felt to be essential. Instead of thinking as if systems behind or below or above our immediate interaction are causing our actions, this series is proposing that we think as participants in the patterning process of interaction itself as the movement of experience. By thinking within our participative action, we must turn in our search for causes to the paradoxical nature of our experience of human relating. This, then, brings our attention to the way we are continuously constructing the future together as the movement of sense-making in the present. The potential for both stability and change is arising between us as the constraints of history are reshaped spontaneously, changing the meaning of the past *and* the future in the immediate experience of relating as embodied persons.

Learning to learn

This mapping of 'structured processes' as systems of human interaction, which has been the mainstay of OD activity, has brought its own questions and issues. One troubling issue was our very humanness itself, our unpredictability, our emotional irrationality, our fears, doubts, illusions and intuitions, which seemed to get in the way of the kind of rational inquiry OD was advocating. Let us look at how another influential practitioner and writer, Chris Argyris, struggled with some of these difficulties:

> The validity of inquiry in the action context is threatened by a variety of defensive routines, including self-censorship and face saving. Our research indicates that human beings, when dealing with threatening issues, typically act in ways that inhibit generation of valid information and that create self-sealing patterns of escalating error.
>
> (Argyris, Putman and Smith, 1985: 61)

What was to be done about this? The problem was seen to lie with the individual learning process, understood as a reasoning process:

> It is important that we strive to correct the factors at the individual level so that when we turn to redesigning organizations, the activity is not dominated by culturally induced constraints and by tacit fears related to organizations going out of control. It makes sense, therefore, to begin with individuals and to examine the way they reason about action.
>
> (Argyris, 1982: 14)

This is how Argyris himself reasons about this reasoning process:

> If people can choose to be unpredictable, then how will we ever develop a science of human action with which we can predict and generalise? What makes this dilemma solvable is that people cannot normally be unpredictable to themselves. They must design and execute the actions that others will experience as unpredictable. This means that actions are designed. Behind every major action is a process of reasoning, no matter how automatic and spontaneous the action appears to be. For example when we ask people to reflect on outbursts, they are able to give the reasoning behind them. To do so means that they can retrieve programs in their heads. It is these programs which inform our actions that we must understand and change if errors are to be corrected in ways that make it unlikely they will recur. Our task therefore, is to discover the reasoning processes people use to make themselves unpredictable. . . . In order to design

their actions, they must have some theory in their heads about what and how to design. I hope to show that they do have such theories in their heads – that if we understood the theory, we would be able to predict when they will be unpredictable and the limits of what they will design to be unpredictable.

(Argyris, 1982: 14)

Argyris devoted himself as a practitioner to the task of helping people close the gap between their 'espoused theories' and their 'theories-in-use'. This idea assumes that tacit theories of action exist out of awareness of the same kind as explicit theories of action. In other words that a rational inquiry into the basis of our actions can yield causal explanations of a particular kind, based on either cause–effect relationships or on identifying 'rules of engagement' that unfold certain kinds of outcome. This is no easy matter as 'A full specification of the theories of action held by any individual would be enormously lengthy and complex' (1985: 83) and 'Human beings can be understood to act according to rules that they cannot state' (ibid.: 82). Argyris developed painstaking methods, akin to double-entry book-keeping, for surfacing these tacit maps and changing them to provide us with much better tools for designing the future. This was his contribution to the design of an effective goal-directed learning process which 'engages human agents in public self-reflection in order to change the world'. These methods involved intensive cycles of inquiry of a cooperative kind amongst groups of practitioners. Thus people tried to construct mappings of what was *really* informing and guiding their actions, instead of what they *said* or *believed* was guiding them. Thus they could learn to design and produce more effective action. They could map and re-engineer their own 'mental models' in what came to be known as 'double-loop learning' or 'learning to learn'.

Argyris became rather pessimistic about our capacity to engage in the kind of collective learning processes he advocated without ever abandoning his essential premises. He saw human beings as 'skilled incompetents', addicted to what he called 'Model 1 learning', in which we interact in ways aimed at preserving control, avoiding embarrassment and loss of face, seeking to preserve a current sense of self-in-the world. He wanted us to discover Model 2 learning through which we are willing to experience the discomfort and vulnerability occasioned by being openly curious and exposing ourselves to the risk of becoming different. However, as I have tried to show, Argyris has dismissed spontaneous, unpredictable, emergent change in our current sense of self-in-the-world and does not understand this as emerging communicatively between us rather than 'in' individual's minds intentionally choosing to change through insight into their own 'mental patterns'. So he is forced to pursue an arduous and exhausting 'mining' of experience for elaborate propositions and explanations for actions and their underlying motivations, ignoring any idea that this kind of interaction might be an ongoing creation more than an uncovering of what was 'there'. Process reviews conducted at the end of meetings and exercises introduced to surface and change frames of reference, or 'mindsets', are commonplace tools for introducing learning processes that are informed by this heritage.

Donald Schon worked closely with and evolved Argyris's ideas to emphasize more clearly the constructivist nature of the relationship between the knowing practitioner and the world he or she knows. He understood professional artistry of any kind as involving 'world-making' – the countless acts of attention, inattention, naming, sense-making, boundary setting and control that the practitioner makes moment by moment:

> Professionals are in transaction with their practice worlds, framing the problems that arise, framing their roles and constructing practice situations to make their role frames operational. They hold reflective conversations with the materials of their situations and thus remake part of their practice world, *revealing the usually tacit processes of world-making that underlie all of their practice*.
>
> (Schon, 1987: 30, my italics)

Like Argyris, Schon holds that reflection can surface descriptions of tacit knowing so that it becomes possible to *direct* this process in which tacit knowing and articulate sense-making are inextricably bound together. I would say that this ideal of the 'reflective practitioner' is the one that mostly continues to grip our imaginations and shape our aspirations to be effective and competent individual practitioners engaged in life-long learning. Instead, I have been asking what happens when spontaneity, unpredictability and our capacity to be surprised by ourselves are *not* explained away but kept at the very heart of an account of the evolution of sense-of-self-in-the-world.

The learning organization

Exactly the same ways of thinking that shape individual learning practice also shapes approaches to collective learning or the learning organization. Thus Schein's complicated network of intersecting cultural norms is understood by Peter Senge in terms of a relatively small number of 'system archetypes' which managers can learn to recognize. These simplify the dense web of shifting conflicting norms, into a smaller number of opposing tensions that create a dynamic that is repetitive. All systems in Nature are understood in terms of self-reinforcing growth processes in interplay with limiting conditions which constrain growth. Having identified and mapped these processes, managers can nurture growth and mitigate limiting processes at key points of leverage. This is the 'fifth discipline' of systems thinking that Senge (1990) advocated in his influential book of the same title:

> the reason that structural explanations are so important is that only they address the underlying causes of behaviour at a level that patterns of behaviour *can be changed*. Structure produces behaviour, and changing underlying structures can produce different patterns of behaviour.
>
> (Senge, 1992: 53, author's italics)

Again we are offered ways to help people in organizations observe, assess and collaboratively change the self-regulating processes in which they find themselves repetitively engaged. This discipline involves yet a further rising above the rising above that Schein's 'simplifying models' involve. Many other forms of practice rely on a similar strategy. The work of Charles Hampden-Turner (1994) and Fons Trompenaars (1993), for example, relies on identifying key tensions or dilemmas that characterize whole national or corporate cultures. Thus managers are asked to rise even further above or dig even deeper to surface a number of different value systems and see how circular processes in each give rise to different patterns. They are then in a position to take up multiple perspectives or see through multiple lenses at a number of different 'systemic wholes'. This process of learning from the past in terms of sophisticated tools for identifying and assessing whole patterns is then used for designing more desirable whole patterns.

This is the mode of thought that largely informs the professional activity of organization development and strategic leadership. Although organizations are acknowledged to be highly intricate, they can be represented by maps of complex feedback interactions between various factors and variables in which formative causation can be traced, and so large-scale changes in the system as a whole can be planned. OD then, promises the possibility of purposeful design of organized wholes, by intervention in the human processes of learning. Demanding as it does a whole system overview as a basis for effective intervention in that system, it sustains a conundrum at its very core. We are asked to think how we might be able to regulate the very process we are invited to understand ourselves as regulated by. No wonder the processes of facilitation and enabling leadership nurtured by this way of thinking can often seem subtly controlling. It is hard to get at this difficulty from within this way of conceptualizing what is going on between us. Thus we may find it very difficult to deal with the unease and vague frustration we may periodically feel as we try to deal with our world of human action in these terms. The conviction that rational self-conscious reflection undertaken cooperatively can always improve our organizational institutions always seems to shy away from dealing with issues of power, control and potential destructiveness.

Group relations

Bennis (1979), writing at the end of the first decade when OD emerged and began to gain credibility as a profession, had already noticed a fundamental deficiency in models of change associated with OD. What he called the 'truth-love model' was paramount, one that assumes that organizations need to be based on conditions of trust, truth telling, consensus and collaboration to be effective. OD could, he believed, claim success in closed bureaucratic systems, in which he included all industry, but not in diffuse, pluralistic power situations and in conditions of mistrust, conflict and even violence. Although troubled, he is unable to offer answers to the dilemma he sees. His final comment on his own position is particularly telling:

> The OD consultant strives to use power that is based on rationality, valid knowledge, and collaboration and to discount power based on and channelled by fear, irrationality and coercion. The latter kind of power leads to augmented resistance to change, unstable changes, and dehumanised irrational conflicts.
>
> (ibid.: 79)

It has been the psychoanalytic practitioners, particularly the Tavistock School of Group Relations, who took up these dilemmas and offered a Freudian perspective on the irrational and unconscious conflicts of the individual psyche writ large in the dynamics of group and organizational life. This offers a welcome counterpoint to the insistent rationality, and occasional naïvety of some OD practice, embracing as it does the human experiences of envy, rivalry, rage, greed, dread, dreams, illusions, sexuality, ambivalence in the face of dependency, the desire to control and much more. This deserves far more consideration than I intend to give here. Although in some ways psychoanalytic approaches have led to organizational practice that seems so different in what it is prepared to deal with, it does not depart in essential ways from approaches that I have already explored. These practitioners also take a 'structured' approach to process, inviting people in organizations to reflect on the underlying patterns, such as 'Oedipal conflicts', 'scapegoating', 'splitting', 'pairing' that are driving observable behaviour and 'getting in the way' of 'task performance.' The approach remains structural in the sense that understanding the complexities of organizational experience is deemed to involve collective reflection to recognize instances of persistent underlying structured dynamics. These are overlayed with the immediate situational particulars of a given context, identifying the parts all are playing in creating the recognized dynamic. These underlying patterns are understood to originate in the interplay of individuals' early histories unconsciously at work in the present. The explanations for what is happening is located in unconscious systems of instinctual drives and social introjects that shape the motivations of interacting individuals. The special contribution of Tavistock consultants lies in their ability to offer appropriate 'interpretations' in terms of these unconscious processes to help people make a particular kind of sense of their experience in terms of a particular explanatory framework. Organizational members are invited to learn to use such interpretations themselves to better understand and handle themselves in potentially destructive organizational processes.

Again and again as practitioners account for their practice, I have shown how they point to identifiable whole patterns (mental models, systems archetypes, scripts, the unconscious, culture), as dynamic structures underlying, explaining and causing our current experience of direct interaction. This way of making sense necessarily constitutes a practice in which all concerned invest themselves in reflexively creating and using such mapping processes as ways of identifying the self-organizing dynamic wholes in which they are participating, so as to reconfigure the interactions that construct the future. This is different from the sense-making practice I have been describing which draws attention to the self-organizing reconfiguring of enabling constraints in direct interaction, in which we make full use of all the maps of our devising as tools of communication. It is the communicative interaction patterning itself that

I am drawing attention to as the paradoxical transformative causal process of constructing the future. The first way of making sense is what this series refers to as 'systemic self-organization', the second is what we have called 'participative self-organization'.

Gestalt

I trained for five years as a Gestalt practitioner and the way I reflect now on this as a sense-making practice illustrates this distinction I am making. The Gestaltists have always been interested in conceiving of experience as a continuous flow of shifting awareness, yet their further theorizing continues in terms of maps and wholes. Awareness becomes again a mysterious flow that 'is an ongoing process, readily available at all times. . . . It is always there – ready to be tapped into when needed . . . furthermore, focussing on one's awareness keeps one absorbed in the present situation' (Polster and Polster; 1973). What puzzled me was what was going on, then, when we were not focussing on or tapping into awareness? Apparently we are leaving absorption in the present by remembering or fantasizing or intellectualizing. Once again we have an ongoing mysterious flow and a map we impose upon the flow, which they called the 'cycle of experience'. This is a model of phases – sensing, awareness, mobilization, action, contact, assimilation, withdrawal, and so on – which maps a stable repetitive dynamic, that of arousal/discharge of 'energy' as 'figures' of gathering interest develop against a 'background' of decreasing interest. The differentiation of figure and ground is then conceptualized as emerging simultaneously from an undifferentiated 'field'. In other words, we have again differentiated concepts brought together as a unity by postulating a third whole – that of a field, which was conceptualized in terms brought from the natural sciences as fields of intra-psychic, inter-personal, inter-group 'forces'. Even at the time, I found field theory as it was conceptualized in Gestalt singularly unconvincing. The map of the 'cycle of experience' orientates practitioners in a particular way (Nevis, 1987). It suggests they pay attention to 'good contact' and to identify 'interruptions to contact' as 'boundary disturbances'. It posits 'wholes of experience', created by completing phases of work within cycles of work so that 'unfinished business' is not accumulated. 'Closure' becomes very important.

> Contact is the experience from which meaning is extracted; resolution is the act of extracting meaning and recognising that closure has occurred, and that the situation is finished or complete. Once meaning

is extracted, we can say that learning has occurred . . . what has been learned becomes part of the ground and is available for later use.

(Nevis, 1987: 29)

In some odd way, this method of making sense instrumentalizes awareness, experience and meaning making. I always found these formulations confusing. They always begged a question that I found difficult to formulate. I now understand the question as, 'What is it we are supposed to be making meaning *of*, or extracting meaning *from* that is changed by meaning making?' Nevis was the main author I knew at the time who was formulating a Gestalt perspective on organizational work. I was actually learning Gestalt practice as a regular experience of interaction in a group of changing membership coming together over a period of many years with Petruska Clarkson (1992) as a teacher. She had what seemed then an odd way of teaching that appealed to me. Whenever she went over a concept she never introduced it the same way twice. If there were supposed to be models and maps there, then they refused to sit still, to the great frustration of some members of her training group. When she made sense with a model she regularly proceeded to make nonsense with it. Often people suggested that she was helping us not to literalize the maps, helping them become tacit, assimilated out of awareness. This, they said, was facilitating the move from conscious to unconscious competence, that distinguishes the experienced practitioner from the novice who is forever consulting the 'how to' instructions. However, when I think back I like to think of her as someone who didn't make sense with maps, however much she enjoyed playing with them as tools of communication. What I learned over these years was to pay attention to the responsive gesturing of communicative interaction in which my experience of myself-amongst-others was always recapitulating and yet shifting, the paradoxical movement into what Griffin calls the 'known-unknown'.

From 'hard' to 'soft' systems

Many system practitioners would argue that the kind of questions I have raised about the mapping and modelling of organizing processes as systemic patterns of relationship and communication have been addressed by the move from 'hard' to 'soft' systems methodologies (Churchman, 1968; Checkland, 1981) and from first to second order research methodologies (von Foerster, 1992). In this move, 'systems' are understood to be social constructs, they are not understood as 'maps' of any kind of real territory. Instead they become ways of picturing the social practices, culture and politics of those drawing the 'system of interest', and developing intentions and making decisions in relation to that system. Soft systems methodologies do not seek to study objective facts or search for causal relations because they view systems as the creative mental constructs of the human beings involved in a process of learning about the divergent ways they are construing their situation. Soft systems methodologies offer a disciplined way to explore the subjective viewpoints and the intentions of all involved in a situation. Systems intervention is an investigation of the process of designing the intervention itself and the culture and politics this process involves. Systems thinking becomes a theory of the observer, rather than the observed. Systems practices involve developing 'rich pictures' of people's understanding of a situation including the history and wider context in which such understanding has developed. Specific models of systems to explicate those worldviews in specific situations are then created, rather than trying to identify the 'truth' about the nature of systems. These models are not blueprints for the design of an objective system but conceptual models contributing to a fuller debate about change. Systems practice in these terms becomes a way of helping people 'picture' their socially created world. The emphasis here is on using and developing such picturing (systemic models) skills to promote thoughtful discussion about action. However, the kind of thought being enabled here is still that of rational frameworks for representing completed patterns of relations for our reasoning gaze to comprehend as an overview. This contrasts with Shotter's approach explored in Chapter 3 in which key aspects of socially constructed realities are 'the unpicturable imaginary'. Like Shotter, I am striving to stay with processual thinking which is always incomplete because of the very nature of the dialogically structured conversational realities emerging in reciprocally responsive relationships between living embodied persons.

Having explored so far the main strands that seem to me to have shaped OD practice, I would like to turn to more specific recent developments of practice. In the last decade or so the conversation about organizational change has been enriched by exchanges between practitioners in different fields. There has also been much discussion about the significance of a world where people's lives are vastly more interconnected, and where they are far more aware of their diversity and interdependence than ever before. I will look at a number of these developments seen as responses to an understanding of organizations in terms of networks of complex interdependencies and interactions. These are:

- involving diverse and sometimes large numbers of people in intensive 'whole system' events such as 'Future Search Conferences' and 'Open Space Technology' around initiatives of concern to all involved.
- moving towards a practice of managing organizations as 'living systems'.
- educating people in the 'art of dialogue'.
- designing the social infrastructure to identify and nurture 'communities of practice'.

All these approaches are working with concepts of participation, conversation and sense-making, so I will draw attention to the different kinds of logic, different metaphors and different narratives of change that inform these different approaches. I will try to show how concerns which may at first seem very close to my own may lead in different directions and I ask what kind of consequences in practice these differences may have.

7 What's the difference?
other approaches to conversation, participation and organizational change

- 'Getting the whole system in the room'
- Organizations as 'living systems'
- The art of dialogue
- Communities of practice

When I began working with organizations twenty-five years ago, it still seemed a sensible proposition that the task of leaders was to have a good overview, a grasp of the big picture, the real state of affairs which enabled them to direct and co-ordinate the activity of an enterprise. It went without saying that this view was superior, was indeed 'global', that it subsumed other, more local views. However over this period such hubris has been tempered by the experience of the world as more complex and less directly manageable. The image of the generals occupying an elevated position on a hill so that they could survey the coming battlefield, develop strategies and brief the troops, gave way to images of leadership more distributed amongst task forces, action teams and special project groups exploring the way forward. Horizons were no longer clearly visible. The idea was to metaphorically send out scouting parties to get a glimpse of what might be around the next corner, or over the next hill. Leaders were meant to ensure that their organizations were well prepared to take advantage of possible future scenarios. Competitive advantage involved 'getting to the future first' (Hamel and Prahalad, 1994). Despite considerable uncertainty, people could develop confidence that they would be able to find out about eventualities likely to matter, in time to respond to them effectively. Although this metaphor of organizational leadership is still prevalent, Lane and Maxfield (1996) point out that in the last decade or so the 'horizons' are now experienced in even more complex ways. The territory of exploration is increasingly understood by managers as not actually 'there' but being formed by the exploration itself. This is the new riddle posed for the mapping way of sense-making that has held sway for so long. It is difficult to map ground that moves with every step of the explorers, creating a different experience of uncertainty. 'Since their destination is always beyond their current foresight horizons in time, the connection between what they decide to do and where they are going is always tenuous and hence ambiguous. They inhabit a world of emergence, perpetual novelty and ambiguity.' Perhaps this underplays the possibility that this uncertainty also produces experiences of recognition and familiarity that may be comforting or frustrating, but nonetheless it is an image with which many managers I work with find resonance.

Griffin (2001) makes a similar point about the shift in flow or process metaphors. We may imagine ourselves as leaders standing by the side of a stream, planning and controlling a boat's passage between the banks. We may shift to imagining ourselves on the boat navigating through hazards and helpful currents with reference to fixed points on the banks. Or we may imagine ourselves as an inseparable part of the turbulent movement of the stream itself, patterning the flow of our experience as we make sense together.

The global overview from the hill, the solid ground of the bank with its fixed reference points, is lost to us. In an economic world that increasingly talks of globalization, we are all local now.

It is this increasing convergence on ideas of complexity, diversity, plurality and interdependence in a socially constructed world of human action that is leading many organizational practitioners to attend to and work with the self-organizing, self-referential sense-making interactions of people as the key processes of organizational stability and change. In the following sections I turn to several such approaches. I point to what seems very similar in the kind of concerns and issues that practitioners advocating these approaches take up. At the same time, I draw particular attention to how these practitioners *account for or explain* what they are doing in different ways. I ask how these different ways of making sense shift what is experienced as important, what really matters and so where the weight of attention, energy and resources of other kinds comes to lie.

'Getting the whole system in the room'

Carefully designed and facilitator-led large group events are an increasingly popular example of 'intervention' into the ongoing processes of organizing. These are intensive interactive conferences intended to stimulate new forms of action to address ambitious change in complex situations. Participants are invited to identify issues and create self-managing small groups to generate proposals for further work. The result is a public plan of action. The events are intended to mobilize highly-energized collaborative temporary communities during the event itself which, it is hoped, will sustain subsequent activity. The starting point is often the need to transform a messy, conflictual situation in which complex interactions between numerous diverse stakeholders are creating a situation that is unsatisfactory in the eyes of some at least. For example, 'despite much expenditure, effort and commitment, healthcare access in this town remains patchy', or 'as a result of disjointed activity in silos we are failing to capture market opportunities'. The working concept is to bring a microcosm of the whole complex system together and create the conditions that foster spontaneous reorganization into more aligned, goal-directed activity. These methodologies are heralded as major advances in large system or whole system interventions, capable of producing rapid change. I will look at two in particular, Open Space Technology and Future Search Conferencing.

In a way these approaches are providing opportunity for 'making sense of gathering and gathering to make sense' as I described in Chapter 2, but there are important differences. Primary among these is that when practitioners explain what they see as the value of these methods, they seem to suggest that self-organization can be sponsored and harnessed, however subtly, to good ends in the interests of all concerned. It is uncomfortable to raise questions about whether this is ever possible as the convictions and values of those concerned in promoting these methodologies are always overwhelmingly positive. Harrison Owen (1992), originator of Open Space Technology, talks of releasing love as the generating force in the workplace. Weisbord and Janoff, writing about Future Search say 'anyone who organises a "whole system in the room" meeting contributes to the betterment of all of us' (2000: 198). The way these practitioners account for their work suggests that we can marshal a whole system of concern or a microcosm that reflects it, and operationalize good intentions for that whole.

Open Space Technology

Open Space Technology (OST) was developed by Harrison Owen (1992). Owen later talks of the genesis of OST as residing in four organizing ideas. These are the geometry of the circle (meeting in the round), the rhythm of the breath (iterative cycles of working issues), and the two mechanisms of the marketplace (organizing around different interests) and the bulletin board (public posting of who is meeting where about what) (1997: 6). He sees these organizing ideas as universal motifs of productive human communication. He is paying attention to stable patterns of human relating across history and cultures. In so doing I would point out that other, just as stable patterns of human interaction such as secret deals, patronage, power plays and so on are not being focussed on. Also, over time what all these patterns of human interaction give rise to may be judged both good and ill by different people making sense afresh of what has gone before.

Participants join the event on the basis of their interest in the question announced as the key task of the Open Space event. Once there, they have the opportunity to articulate to the public forum issues and topics of concern, related to the theme being explored. In so doing they are undertaking to lead a small working group of any others responding to this topic. The topics are logged on a large board indicating meeting slots that will take place at specified times and places over the period of the conference. People organize themselves around these topics, moving between groups as interest and capacity to contribute evolves, revisiting and reorganizing the bulletin board as the event progresses. The output of each working group is noted and pinned up by each topic owner and collated into collective output at the end of the event.

What sounds similar?

Participating in an Open Space event and joining working groups is based on people self-selecting themselves according to the strength of their interest and capacity to contribute. The work is conceived as a collective inquiry process. People organize themselves to identify, lead and contribute to issues of concern to them related to the overall aim of the Open Space event and to work them in whatever way they want, culminating in proposals and agreements for taking further action beyond the conference. The design is based on an iterative process of gathering, making sense, dispersing and gathering again in different configurations, creating opportunities for exchange, unexpected connections, involvement, learning, cross-fertilization, new ideas and possibilities for new action. Although the output is recorded and collated, no attempt is made to develop an overall picture.

What's different?

The signal that draws people to an OST event, says Owen, must be a clearly focussed question: 'For OST to work, it must focus on a real business (or community) issue that is of passionate concern to those who will be involved' (1997: 20). By 'real' here is meant 'widely-recognized'. Formulating a clear question with the sponsors of the Open Space, and disseminating the invitation to gather together those with a stake in working the issues raised by the question, is thus something that OST practitioners invest effort in doing. Having helped the sponsors send out an engaging signal, the role of the facilitators of Open Space is then to 'host' and 'hold' the open space as a container with a simple structure, rules of engagement and clear boundaries within which the participants organize themselves. They do not join in the sense-making process at the event. Their political engagement involves two aspects: their alliance with the sponsors who have formulated the nature of the inquiry, and the way their design channels activity towards public action plans in the service of that legitimated purpose. A lot of emphasis is placed on the recording and collating of output from small groups and the conference as a whole. This tangible output, a thick book of 'stuff', is emphasized by Owen as important for people to feel in a tangible way the productivity of the event. This, then, is an open space in which an overarching theme that makes sense of people's presence and their interaction has already been set. What Owen seems to mean by the event 'working' is that substantial action plans which make sense to those who developed them are generated in the service of this theme between people motivated to pursue them. What OST offers is a legitimate opportunity for intensive networking of a directed kind. In the tradition of OD as I described in the last chapter, it is a highly interactive goal-directed, action-oriented learning process. Although the structure and facilitation may seem light and minimal, it would be naïve not to notice the potency of the design for containing anxiety. It is challenging to compose one's ideas into a short statement or question that might invite others to join you in working further. It feels daunting and exposing for some to express this in a public forum and pin up their invitation on the board, waiting to see whether others will ignore or respond to their invitation, in the market place of interest. However, this is a designed process whereby everyone is asked to do the same thing at the same time. The facilitators emphasize such 'rules of engagement' as 'whoever turns up are the right people' and a generally benign attitude that whatever happens is of value. If, for example, you don't want to stay in a group and wander around, or develop ad hoc corridor conversations, then you are fulfilling the sanctioned role of cross-pollinator. The bulletin board structures the day into working sessions of specified duration from which output in the recommended format is expected. It is possible to track what is going on where and amongst whom, and we all finish up together with a wad of collated material to take away as evidence of our endeavours and what may come of them. This is what people often mean by a stimulating but 'safe', well-managed working environment, in which structure and purpose are clear, difference does not seem so threatening, and a satisfying sense of collective productivity flowers. Such experiences tend to engender enthusiasm and goodwill, a sense of mutual value, a strengthening of one's identity as a contributor to collective effort and increased motivation for taking future action. This, I think, is what leads Owen to talk optimistically about organizational processes that generate and are generated by 'love'. The design, pace and facilitation of Open Space conspire to offer people the opportunity to co-create briefly the dynamics of a highly active, apparently very productive working community in which the experience of fellow-feeling tends to flourish. The implication of Owen's writing is that organizing could/should be more like this more of the time. I cannot argue with this aspiration as a human desire, but I question whether the conditions that enable this quality of fellow-feeling can ever be more than temporary.

In the previous chapters I have been describing my attempts to work intentionally as an organizational practitioner/facilitator with situations where there is far less clarity of design, purpose, structure, boundaries or rules of the game, situations which are far closer in fact to the 'everyday life' of organizational work. Open Space practitioners help to co-construct temporary power relations in which these constraints are held clear in a similar way for all, enabling rapid work of a certain kind within those constraints. In contrast I have been asking what is involved in participating in those interactive processes in which multiple ways of making sense of what we are doing are more obviously in play simultaneously. I am interested in the way conflicting themes which are organizing our experience of working together emerge, propagate and change in the ongoing conversations in which I participate. I am not trying to gather in one place a 'microcosm of the whole', where a clear 'system of interest' has been identified, but rather working as part of loose webs of relationship both legitimate and spun through a multitude of other kinds of relating. The Open Space event generates a strong temporary sense of community, whereas the kind of work I am describing generates a rather weaker, shifting, ill-defined sense of 'us' because conversations are always following on from previous conversations and moving on into further conversations involving others. People are often gathering and conversing around ill-defined issues, legitimation is often ambiguous, motivation is very varied. The work has much less clear and well-managed beginnings and endings, there is not the same sense of creating common ground for new concerted action. There is no pre-conceived design for the pattern of work; it evolves live. We are not necessarily trying to create outputs in the form of public action plans; rather, we are making further sense of complex situations always open to further sense-making, and in so doing redirecting our energies and actions. I have been describing a process of encouraging narrative sense-making as a fellow participant, different among other differences. That includes telling the stories that make sense of my own participation and joining the conversation that continues to construct further meaning together of the stories we are telling and hearing. My political engagement, with all the questions this raises, is akin to that of the people I am working with. What matters, because of the way I am making sense, are the political processes by which legitimate purpose arises and transforms unpredictably through ongoing activity. I am not setting out to make situations 'safe' for others. Rather I am interested in learning, with others, how we may live at times with a somewhat less 'safe' sense of self, as we experience changing and being changed by our sense-making interactions, as the enabling constraints we are mutually sustaining undergo spontaneous shifts. This is a capacity I think we need to strengthen in the increasingly fluid world of today's organizations and I am linking it to developing increasing appreciation for the craft of participation as self-organizing sense-making.

Future Search

Future Search conferences were developed by Weisbord and colleagues (1992) from the earlier work of Trist and Emery (1973) at the Tavistock

Institute. Here again a group of sponsors prepare to take the lead in organizing a future search event by agreeing on a working title that will be the 'task' of the conference. This task is usually a significant question about how to organize for the future. They consider the widest possible range of stakeholders who might be affected by working on the task, who have information to bring or who might have the authority and resources to act in relation to that task. These are then reduced by the planning group to around eight stakeholder groups who are personally invited to join the conference. Future Search has a generic design over three days, carefully facilitated, that involves everyone in a particular sequence of sense-making activity in particular configurations in and across stakeholder groups that culminates in action planning. The design is predicated on these basic ideas:

- invite the 'whole system' into the room.
- think globally, before acting locally.
- future focus and common ground rather than problem solving and conflict resolution.
- self-management and responsibility for action.

The idea of creating the 'larger picture' remains, although it is now understood as socially constructed rather than really 'out there'. If people can develop a larger picture together in some way it is assumed that they will be better able to integrate their actions to realize a more desired future for this larger picture.

What sounds similar?

Weisbord and Janoff point out how Future Search differs from traditional organization development activity. They say that they are not trying to close a gap between what is and what ought to be. They say that they do not ask conference participants to create or apply any kind of diagnostic framework that leads to the dissonance needed to 'unfreeze' a system and which leads people to want to reorder their relationships and capabilities (2000: 8). They suggest that the introduction of training exercises, structured ice-breakers or diagnostic instruments may reduce the anxiety of participants and facilitators but serves no other useful purpose for this kind of event. They caution that expert input or top-down speeches followed by question-and-answer sessions are a weak strategy for building collaborative action. They discourage lots of advance data gathering and pre-read inputs as necessary to the process of Future

Search (ibid.: 60–61). They say that they are not working to improve
relationships between people or functions as an aim in itself. They do not
try to teach people any special kind of skills to enable them to engage in
the conference process; they say they only need people to 'show up and
use the skills, experience and motivation they already have' (ibid.: 4).
The conference works by engaging people in direct interaction with one
another. They are not aiming for dramatic individual change, but rather
changes in the action potential among individuals, based on discovering
new alignments and possibilities (ibid.: 9).

What's different?

Weisbord and Janoff are working with sense-making processes but their
emphasis on what really matters is again different. They are designing
processes that will enable 'everybody' or as varied a group as possible
consistent with the purpose of the conference to 'improve the whole
system'. They spend time helping sponsor groups identify the task and
the 'right' cross-section of people to invite to the event, and they
emphasize the importance of full attendance for the whole event. I am not
working with the idea of a whole system to be improved and so do not
spend time trying to get 'the system' or a microcosm of it gathered
together at the same time. It is, I believe, the spatial metaphor of 'system'
as map that creates the sense that it is important to have everyone
together at the same time in the same place in order to create the shift in
patterns of interaction that can shift the whole system. This idea creates a
practice of developing and following up highly designed and managed
'events'. My temporal metaphor orientates me to join others involved in
the continuous process of making sense of gathering and dispersing, in
constantly shifting configurations of political and social life in
organizational settings.

Weisbord and Janoff understand change in terms of global patterns
emerging from local interaction, not as a paradoxical process but in terms
of people creating shared visions of desired futures and common ground
for collaborating to achieve them. Only by identifying a desired future
whole consisting of interlocking shared values and goals can people
appreciate the shift in local interaction needed to allow such a future to
emerge. This means that the Future Search design invites people to
construct together trajectories of their own personal histories, global
trends and the history of the particular organization, community or issue,

and to create from this a 'map' of the global context that has emerged from this history of local interaction. Emery and Trist drew on Von Bertalanffy's concept (1952) that everything in nature connects with everything else. The lack of *temporal process* in the way this idea has come to be understood means that we take it for granted that we can map out these connections as a whole pattern, however temporary such a snapshot is understood to be.

People are encouraged to own their contribution to this current larger context in terms of 'prouds' and 'sorries'. The next step is to create as fully as possible a picture of a desired future context that is widely shared. The final step is that of people identifying potential projects and collaborations that will contribute to realizing this envisioned better future. In contrast to this I have been describing work in terms of people making narrative sense of being and working together by responsively weaving stories that make sense of their presence in the communicative action that is evolving. This conversation is reconstructing the past and constructing the future in the sense-making of the present as spontaneous shifts in the patterning of identity and difference. I am describing the experience of mutually sustained constraints that we are holding one another to, and transforming, in our ongoing relating. I am not aiming for a shared map of past, present or future, even though aspiration, desire, fears, prejudices and memories are being expressed throughout the conversation.

Weisbord and Janoff describe the process of Future Search as 'riding an emotional roller-coaster'. The design of the sense-making process has this potential pattern embedded in it. What happens as people construct together a large scale mind-map of current reality as an open system of interdependent trends within and between the search entity and the world outside? They begin to see themselves as caught up in this complex system with accompanying feelings of confusion, hopelessness, frustration, even impotence. However, as they are invited to see this global pattern as emerging from the complexity of local interaction in the past, they are encouraged to 'own' the contribution their part of the system has played in creating the larger picture. The idea that different local interaction could lead to a better future offers the beginning of hope and a sense of being able to make a difference. Enacting, visualizing and articulating a better, indeed ideal, system strengthens the sense of hope and capacity. People are offered the possibility of choosing to contribute to the unfolding of this better future, 'actualizing what is trying to happen', and to make realistic commitments to cooperate towards this, rather than re-enact the conflicts and problems of the past. Publicly-stated commitments increase the potential of mutually sustained expectations. The roller-coaster journey engenders a tension of despair turning to hope turning to realistic choices, which is seen by Weisbord and Janoff as contributing to the transformational process of the Future Search conference.

Again, in the kind of work I have been describing, it is clear that participants experience a wide range of thoughts and feelings, but it is not orchestrated as a collective experience or collective journey in any way. The facilitation that I am interested in involves participating actively in the movement of sense-making as it evolves in ordinary everyday interaction. Compare the 'drama' of the Ferrovia meeting described in Chapter 4 with descriptions of a Future Search 'roller-coaster'.

The emphasis on developing common ground and a shared vision of a desired future as a necessary basis for creating change leads the Future Search practitioners to talk about encouraging difference but not conflict. This means that articulation of differences of opinion, of values, of goals are encouraged, respected, but 'parked'. They are listed separately from the developing shared common ground. In contrast it is precisely in engaging the immediate conflict of taking the next step that I would see the transformation of power relations and enabling/constraints taking place. Weisbord and Janoff are quite explicit about suggesting how differences in a group should be handled. When strong differences of opinion, values or goals are introduced, they look for 'sub-grouping', in other words others who will ally themselves with the speaker and view expressed, so that no one feels isolated or out on a limb. If this does not happen they will find a way to offer support to the person expressing a difference. They are constantly tracking 'differences in apparent similarities' and 'similarities in apparent differences'. The unity of the system in the room is sustained by listening for or offering integrating 'both/and' statements when differences and strong feelings are expressed (ibid.: 180). Thus, anxiety rises as difference is expressed and is contained by acceptance and integration. This is very different from living with the anxiety of the paradoxical nature of identity/difference, inclusion–exclusion *not* resolved by the integration of both/and. I am not seeking to sustain the unified identity of the system in the room when I am working, but to live with others in the paradox that every inclusion is simultaneously exclusionary, every exclusion simultaneously inclusionary, every expression of identity is simultaneously an expression of difference.

The approach to facilitation that is advocated for running successful
Future Search conferences draws very much on the Tavistock tradition.
The facilitators hold the space, where keeping a focus on the stated
purpose of the conference, maintaining the boundaries of task (the
stated purpose of each session) and time (all sessions start and stop
on time) and managing the large group dialogue are considered the
key aspects of the work. They are influenced by Bion's (1961)
psychoanalytic work on repetitive patterns in groups, particularly a
tendency in the face of anxiety to 'fight or flight', dependency and
counter-dependency patterns in relation to authority and scapegoating,
all ways in which the group energies become diverted from working on
the task. Weisbord credits Emery and Trist with the discovery that a
clear task placed in a shared global context reduces anxiety in a group
and thus the tendency to fight or flee. Thus the facilitators do not 'join'
the work of the conference participants; they do and say as little as
possible. Whenever the whole conference gathers for dialogue, they
*make it a point to stay silent as long as it takes for the first person to
say something* (ibid.: 177).

> We keep the door open by listening without acting. We are mindful
> that each time we solve a problem we deprive others of a chance to
> solve it for themselves. Each time we interrupt the action, we pre-
> empt someone else's acting. Just waiting often is all a group needs
> from us to shift towards active dialogue, reality checking and creative
> collaboration.
>
> (ibid.: 158)

Future Search facilitators say they endeavour to sustain a relatively
neutral relationship with conference participants. In fact, their political
alliance is again with the sponsors. One of the boundaries they say they
use their power to hold is to keep the conference task or purpose 'centre
and front'. When I am working, I intentionally participate in the chat of
organizational life, joining conversations in corridors, informally
dropping in on people in offices and taking many a cup of coffee. I also
regularly phone people to talk things over. When I join existing task
forces and working groups, I participate rather than attempt to facilitate
them. I ask questions, voice opinions, make suggestions, interrupt people,
show my responses. Weisbord and Janoff talk about being 'dependable
authorities', meaning that they can be relied upon to 'provide information
people don't have, start and stop on time, reiterate overall goals, manage
large group dialogues so that all views are heard, and back out when the
group is working' (ibid.: 184). They reiterate that it is up to participants

to take responsibility for what they want to do with the space. Their job is to hold the boundaries of that space and the process for moving through it. I do not seek to do either. I actively take up responsibility with others for participating in the often fraught processes by which we are always coming to know ourselves and what we are in the process of doing. To the extent that I have authority by being invited to work in the organization by a usually senior manager, I use it to exemplify and encourage curiosity in and exploration of a continuous inquiry mode – what do we think we are doing here?

The design of both Open Space and Future Search events regularly produces the enthusiasm, collective focus and new action plans that its advocates suggest. The experience often generates optimism and goodwill. What happens after is not examined or written about in any detail. My question is not 'Is this worth doing?' Much may come of such events. Much *will* come of them and this will bear a complex relation to the hopes, fears and aspirations of the participants. My question is how to work with the ongoing conversational life of organizations in which such events may occasionally arise.

Organizations as 'living systems'

Amongst a growing number of organizational practitioners today, the conversation about organizations has changed in a significant way. Instead of just talking about organized wholes and whole systems, people have begun to talk about organizations as 'living systems' or 'living wholes'. There are many aspects of this approach that are very appealing, but it finishes up with a declaration that organizations are in some way 'alive' that, for me, has troubling implications.

Initially there is an evocative appeal to a perspective which is said to be organic, holistic and humane rather than the 'dead' and deadening reductionism of seeing organizations as mechanical systems. In the midst of growing concern about the impact of human technologies and enterprise on the earth's resources, there is also a metaphorical appeal to learning from the economy, creativity and resilience of the natural world, before it gets 'messed up' by human intervention. We are invited to learn from the way Nature organizes and works, by harnessing findings in branches of the natural sciences, particularly evolutionary biology and the complexity sciences. This includes an explicit or implicit ethical appeal to the need to create sustainable business and social justice by seeing human organizations as *part of* rather than *separate from* the ecology of the planet, part of a 'living world'.

In this way of thinking, an organization becomes an autonomous living unity, with emergent properties of the whole, arising from the self-organizing interaction of networks of human individuals and groups, each of which is also an autonomous living unity. Individuals, at one level, and organizations, groups, cultures, ecologies and the planet (as in Lovelock's (1979) Gaia theory) at other levels can all be conceived as autonomous living wholes. This move draws in ideas about the nature of life which integrates the far-from-equilibrium dissipative structures of Prigogine (1984, 1997), the non-linear mathematics of Complexity theory and Maturana and Varela's (1992) theories of the autopoetic network structures of living cells. Writers such as Capra (1996) have shown how these ideas can be brought together to offer an all-encompassing theory of the pattern, structure and process of life in systems terms. An organization can then be understood as a far-from-equilibrium dissipative network structure produced by processes of iterative communicative interactions of a self-referential, autopoetic nature.

The key idea that I want to focus on is what happens as self-organization in the world of human action starts to be seen as producing emergent 'living wholes' with their own integrity of identity and purpose, something with 'a mind of its own'. This move then starts to incorporate notions of the spirit, soul and collective intelligence, wisdom, even of this 'living whole'.

For example, not so long ago I found myself sitting, once again, in a circle of chairs with about thirty other people. A woman was holding a large semi-precious stone and explaining that this particular stone had been used at a number of previous gatherings. It had therefore acquired a special significance as a symbol. The woman spoke in words and tone that invited all those present to share with her the symbolic importance of the stone, to further invest it with significance. There was some suggestion in her words that the stone might be literally imbued in some way with energy and wisdom from previous gatherings. As the stone was handed to someone in the circle they were asked to voice their reflections. When each person had finished he or she got up and gave the stone to another in the circle who had not yet spoken until it had passed to all. No one refused the stone or remained silent with it in their hands. Some spoke briefly, some at length, some personally and emotionally, others more abstractly. It took perhaps two hours to complete this ritual. No one moved from his or her seat, no one spoke twice, no one was interrupted, no one passed comment on what anyone else had said.

What kind of gathering was this? It was a group of senior executives, organizational consultants and researchers exploring together the themes of organizational learning, change and leadership at a workshop convened by SoL – the Society for Organizational Learning. The scene is not unique – many people on seminars of one sort or another might find themselves involved in some variation of this kind of activity, sometimes called the 'talking stick'. It comes from an old tradition of large community gatherings in different cultures where the passing of a special object confers the right to speak and be heard to one person at a time, slowing down proceedings and stilling the potential for confusing babble. This is not just a technique for managing a discussion in a democratic manner. It here aspired to be something more – to evoke a quality of speaking and listening in which some kind of larger wisdom might emerge amongst the group gathered. More than that, there was here the suggestion that the group was tuning itself to a larger intelligence as people experienced themselves as part of a systemic whole, that of humankind, or the living earth or cosmos. This larger wisdom was sometimes referred to as 'memory of the whole' which in turn evokes each person's 'highest self' or allows them to tap their 'deepest levels of knowing' (Brown and Bennett, 1998). The overtones of spiritual practice are what led me to use the word 'ritual' in my description.

I am well aware that many people find such sessions inspiring and would not share my discomfort that there can be something subtly oppressive about this kind of approach. The few occasions I have worked with members of the SoL community, I am aware of how similar our concerns appear to be to create opportunities for conversation between diverse people about the issues that concern and motivate them. Yet the different way we think about what we are doing, and why, does produce significant differences. The kind of conversation that I describe above is very unlike the kind of conversation I have been describing in earlier chapters.

What sounds similar?

Practitioners such as Senge and colleagues (Kofman and Senge, 1993; Senge *et al.*, 1999) who write about organizations as 'living systems' are interested in exploring what we are coming to understand about how living organisms evolve in natural ecologies through complex webs of adaptive relationships. They then ask the question, as we have in this series, what these ideas can mean in the human social world where our experience of self-consciousness and freedom of choice must be taken into account. In Senge's thinking 'learning organizations' as self-organizing systems have become 'learning communities' and then 'communities of commitment'. His question is how people interact to generate joint commitment to enterprises in which their own sense of self is at stake. He points out how learning communities promote change in our very selves since 'to all intents and purposes, most of the time, we *are* our mental models'. He and his colleagues are very alive to the dangers of conformity. They are concerned not to exclude people who disagree so that learning communities do not degenerate into cults. They insist that content and process are inseparable. They advocate organizing around dialogue instead of planning elaborate agendas. They talk about the paradoxes of transformational learning. However, their understanding of the word 'transformational' is quite different from mine.

What's different?

When I talk of transformation, I mean evolving forms of identity, of persons, groups, societies, emerging as we participate in the non-linear processes of human relating, in which both continuity (sameness) and change (difference) occur simultaneously – that is the paradox. When many practitioners who espouse a 'living systems' approach talk of transformation they mean transformation from conflict and fragmentation to *the good* as the cohesion of shared vision and joint purpose.

Senge and Kofman write about leadership of 'communities of commitment' as the 'heart of learning organizations'. The work of such communities is to bring forth new realities and shape the future they deeply desire. They propose that we dissolve frozen patterns of thought that are mindsets generating deeply rooted dysfunctional patterns in our society. These dysfunctions are listed as fragmentation, competition and reactiveness. 'The solvent we propose is a new way of thinking, feeling and being: a culture of systems.' The rather analytical work that Argyris originally proposed for re-examining and changing our 'mindsets' or 'mental models', as I described in the previous chapter, is replaced by a more intuitive, indeed, spiritual approach.

When Senge and colleagues approach sense-making gatherings, they have different work in mind from what I have described in earlier chapters. People are encouraged to voice their aspirations for a better future and to develop a deeply felt commitment to this aspiration, fleshed out as a shared vision. People are also encouraged to articulate frameworks of core values and guiding principles which would 'operationalize' such a future. These are the core values of love (as compassion, fellow-feeling) in the face of difference, wonder (rather than a desire for control) in the face of unpredictability, humility in the face of complexity (all our maps are provisional and must be open to revision). Inevitably, such aspirational conversation tends towards idealizations of community, where the tension of conflict is transcended, diversity embraced, openness and trust become the order of the day.

The idea of people recovering 'the memory of the whole' that I mentioned above means that people are encouraged to develop 'the awareness that wholes precede parts'. This will make fragmentary thinking systemic. Discovering 'the community nature of the self' turns competition into cooperation: 'I cannot be me without you'. Reactiveness becomes creativeness when we see 'the generative power of language' to bring forth fresh distinctions from the undivided flow of life. In *The Web of Life*, Capra (1996) talks about the shift from the parts to the whole as characteristic of systems thinking. Kofman and Senge say that, 'In the new systems world view, we move from the primacy of the pieces to the primacy of the whole, from absolute truths to coherent interpretations, from self to community, from problem-solving to creating' (1993: 6). I would say that they are proposing a shift that understands wholes formatively causing parts, communities and cultures formatively causing selves, cognitive maps formatively causing the worlds of our experience through languaging. Leadership then becomes our ability to reshape these wholes closer to our deeply felt desire. Once again this involves the rational/formative split causality of Kantian dialectical thinking that we have been questioning in this series.

Since I am not accounting for my work in the same way I do not emphasize attempts to shape the self-organizing systems or wholes in which we are participating. Instead I am thinking in terms of the everyday conflict of taking the next step, as we participate in the ongoing patterning processes of communicative action in which identity and difference of persons in society are always emerging simultaneously. When I describe working with the spontaneous processes of continuity and change, I am not working with Kofman and Senge's core question,

'How do such leadership communities, form, grow and become influential in moving large communities forward?' My questions are: 'How are we are making sense of ourselves and how do we go on from here?' When I describe gathering people in a self-organizing way, it is not by asking a bold and penetrating question or by gathering those 'with a predisposition' for a systems perspective. The gatherings I refer to are people coming together through the connections, associations and multiple motivations arising in their work. When I describe the messy sense-making conversations which shift the enabling constraints people are recreating through relating, this is very different from engaging in 'intensive and open-ended community building activities'. When I describe the new developments which emerge over time, I am not referring to special dialogue projects or learning lab projects which are attempting to grow a special culture or activity in a protected or hot-house situation.

At the gathering I mentioned above, Claus Otto Scharmer talked about his ideas for a new understanding of leadership which he referred to as 'sensing and actualizing emerging futures'. Examining what he means by this illustrates in some detail the kind of thinking that the 'living systems' approach seems to be developing as an understanding of emergence in human communities of commitment.

Scharmer (2000) distinguishes between two *different* sources or processes of learning and argues that *both* are required for organizations to succeed. He calls the first 'reflecting on the experiences of the past' and he calls the second 'sensing and embodying emergent futures' *rather than* re-enacting the patterns of the past. This immediately signals the 'both/and' nature of his thinking, and the particular view he takes of time. His view is that of linear time moving from the past through the present to the future, with one kind of learning relevant to understanding the past and another relevant to creating the future. He talks about *uncovering* ever deeper levels of the structuring nature of the past and bringing this into awareness as a process of presencing. The future is understood as an emerging transcendent whole to be accessed in an essentially mystical manner through bringing it also into presence. This presencing of both past and future is an essentially timeless experience, a fertile void, which he calls generative learning. The present therefore quite explicitly has no time structure and presencing is *manifesting in awareness* what lies beneath or above or behind our experience of direct interaction. In contrast in this series we have been talking about the time structure of a living present by which we mean our lived experience of the movement of experience. This is our experience of direct interaction as we reconstruct the past and construct the possibilities of the future by the same process of complex responsive relating.

Scharmer says that the key challenge for leaders is how to enable teams to uncover layers of reality that will move them from more superficial levels of reflection on the past to generative learning, and he proposes a methodology for doing this. Generative learning is understood as a cycle of seeing, sensing, presencing and enacting and the cognitive process involved is intuition, described as the highest quality of attention, in which Scharmer says that individual intention is at one with the intention of the emerging whole as it comes into presence. It is a process of bringing the emerging whole into reality 'as *it* desires' rather than as the ego desires. Generative learning, as presencing, is a collective forming, enacting and embodying of common will. Will formation involves envisioning understood as enhancing the quality of aspiration, vision and intention and is said to be at the heart of leadership. Presencing is a process of becoming aware, which involves suspension, redirection and letting go. Suspension means taking off one's self-created cognitive filters. Redirection is turning inward to the source of oneself and redirecting attention from current reality (the object) to an emergent reality (the coming-into-being of the object). Next there is letting go, defined as emptying or surrendering to a deeper, higher collective will. Scharmer then adds another stage which he calls 'letting come'. For him, surrender means switching from looking for to letting come, receiving that which is attempting to manifest or that which one is capable of letting manifest. Letting come is a phase of quickening or crystallization in which one allows something to enter. This is the arrival of the highest possible future, the highest presence, the highest Self. What is received is an emerging heightened quality of will and a more tangible vision of what the individual and the group want to create. He describes this as a switch from seeing objects to sensing the field out of which objects and behaviours are enacted. It enables one to understand in a moment the *whole system* and how it is reproducing events and troubling symptoms. This is Scharmer's understanding of the power of intuition – as glimpsing the transcendent whole that one is co-creating through one's own participation.

Enacting is then a further phase of social activity of people all acting in differentiated ways from their highest inner selves now attuned to a deeply shared purpose. Embodying is the incorporation of such enactments into procedures and routines that sustain a desired reality.

Note how Scharmer uses the 'both/and' logic to resolve the paradox of individual/group, by asserting a process by which individual differences now interact to unfold a common desired future. There is difference at the level of the individual and unity at the level of the group because essentially meditative practices have 'attuned' the selves to the unfolding of a commonly desired future, a common good. It is also implied that this common good can also be attuned to the larger good of the larger wholes in which this particular community is embedded.

The language is strikingly mystical. Presencing is described as going through the eye of the needle, a birth, a breaking through a membrane. Scharmer describes it as a mystery and says that it is a mode of relating in which the individual relates to the collective whole of the community, team and organization. In this state people become more 'selfless and become aligned with their true selves and with the intention of the emerging whole. The self is an open gate through which new social substance passes as transformation.' Although he does not refer to Bateson (1973), Scharmer seems to be trying to penetrate the territory where Bateson paused in his postulation of levels of learning. Beyond Level Two learning, the capacity to reflect on the 'mental models' guiding one's actions, Bateson postulated a Level Three learning. He said he could not explain this. He thought it hardly ever happened and the nearest he could come was mystical experience or personal therapy. This is being taken up by Scharmer, when he talks about generative learning as the deepest level of learning and presents it as an essentially mystical experience.

Scharmer defines leadership as the activity of shifting the place from which a system operates and he defines this as shifting the conversation from talking nice and talking tough to reflective and generative dialogues of the kind described above. Generative dialogues lead to an intentional quietness or sacred silence. The only sustainable tool for leading change is the leader's self as the capacity of the 'I' to transcend boundaries of its current organization and operate from the emerging larger whole both individually and collectively. The leader's role is to create the conditions that allow others to shift the place from which their system operates.

Although the two approaches use the same words, therefore, those words have a completely different meaning. I have already noted the different uses of transformation and present/presencing. Participation also means something quite different in the two theories. For Scharmer participation is the immersion of individuals into the collective harmony of human groups attuned to their role in the larger ecology of nature. In complex responsive process theory participation refers to the ordinary everyday communicative interaction between people. Participation is thus not understood as a spiritual mystery but in terms of conversational turn-taking/turn-making and power relating. For Scharmer, emergence means the coming into presence of the transcendent whole while, in complex responsive process theory, it means the self-organization of pattern in communicative interaction between people. For Scharmer, communication is understood as a special form of dialogue, ultimately a sacred silence. In complex responsive process theory the focus of attention is on ordinary everyday conversation and how it constructs social realities.

Sharmer's work spells out the process of thought that accompanies the idea of organizations as Kantian self-organizing systems whose *as if* emergent purposes make sense of the parts and their relationships. The *as if* is literalized in the idea of 'living wholes' with their own consciousness created by the meditative communing of human beings. Leadership becomes the activity of creating 'good' living systems, ideal communities of unified identity at one with the natural world. Griffin (2001) explores in detail in his volume in this series the very important ethical issues facing us as we go down this route. He carefully tracks the implications of Mead's struggle with these issues as he lived through the turbulent years of war and their aftermath in the twentieth century. Mead recognized that idealized values are an essential and precious part of our human heritage. However, he was at pains to point out the danger of trying to implement idealized wholes directly, in other words by suggesting that voluntary commitment to agreed core values as guiding 'rules of behaviour' will unfold these idealized futures. He warns that this process produces a very subtle form of oppression. Scharmer's contribution to a living systems approach seems to go even further in proposing even greater 'surrender' to a good that is trying to happen. Participation comes to mean the willing submission of the 'good self', the highest or idealized self to the wisdom of a collective tuned into a transcendent wisdom. Reluctance to submit to this collectively generated higher purpose is respectfully attributed to the unreadiness of the lower self, the selfish ego. Again, raising doubts about this in the midst of the fervent good intent of practitioners who embrace these ideas is very difficult. Whenever I find myself in gatherings where these kinds of practices are being encouraged in organizational settings I feel deeply uneasy and troubled. A religiosity in a secular age searching for spiritual meaning seems to be embracing a missionary zeal articulated by writers like Wheatley (1992, 1996) and Lewin and Regine (2000) who talk about communities of love and the soul at work. These writers insist that their approach is based on embracing conflict and difference, but in fact they seem to seek to transcend them. I find this disturbing. When I work in organizations, I do not have such aspirations, which does not mean that I do not care about the endless ethical dilemmas in which I am implicated.

The art of dialogue

I have used the word 'conversation' a lot in this book, aware that it has very ordinary connotations. People engage in conversation all through the day, in all sorts of situations, in twos and threes and larger groups. Some conversations are anticipated, prepared for and highly charged, others arise in unlooked for encounters in which concentration may come and go, some conversations seem to flower, others get stuck. The unexpected may arise in the most familiar exchanges, repetition and *déjà vu* in the midst of unusual gatherings. I have been most interested in a certain kind of free-flowing conversation in which themes arise, evolve and shift spontaneously. In this section I want to look at the process of dialogue as a special form of conversation taken up by Isaacs (1999) drawing on the work of the physicist David Bohm. Throughout his life Bohm developed an interest in the way meaning unfolds in collective communication (1987), what he called the 'implicate order' as a way of understanding the nature of 'wholeness' (1980) and the nature of thought as a system (1994). He developed his ideas by initiating and involving himself in numerous gatherings as a living inquiry. Some fifteen to forty people regularly convened in a circle with no pre-set agenda with the aim of sustaining a conversation through which the very processes of thought and consciousness themselves might be revealed in the ordinary processes of relating and communicating. The articulation of elements and principles of dialogue that developed out of this work have been continued by some of those who experienced dialogue with Bohm. This is the Dialogue Project at MIT founded by William Isaacs who has been influential in bringing the ideas and practices into organizational settings and when 'dialogue' is referred to by other practitioners, some form of Bohm's dialogue practice is meant. Dialogue is differentiated from other forms of communication such as debate, discussion or ordinary conversation.

What sounds similar?

I share with advocates of dialogue the experience that open-ended, exploratory conversation amongst attentive, engaged humans is the source of both continuity and change in the patterning of interaction of culture and society. Dialogue is a process of direct interaction that insists 'on facing the inconvenient messiness of daily corporeal experience' (Lee Nichols in Bohm 1999: xi). Bohm talked a lot about the paradox of human introspection, making the point repeatedly that there is no neutral place to stand with which to assess one's own thoughts. He wanted to bring attention to the movement of thought as a 'material process', in other words that thought involves the electrical and chemical activity of brain, nerves, muscles, hormones, blood flow and so on. He was not trying to 'reduce' thought to these processes, but to point out that the movement of thinking is the movement of our bodily experience, much as I have been saying that our sense-making is our experience as bodily selves. This led Bohm to advocate developing attentiveness to the flow of awareness much as Gestalt practitioners have always done, although in his case his work with Krishnamurti, the Indian educator and philosopher, led him to speak of this in terms reminiscent of meditative practices. Isaacs and others, continuing to work with his ideas, are interested in the way that, in the free-flow of dialogue, people find themselves speaking what they did not realize they thought; that there is a quality of listening beyond empathy or sensitivity to others, in which the awareness of the very *mis*-perception of one's spoken intent can lead to new meaning being created on the spot; that new perspectives and possibilities can open spontaneously and unpredictably between people, thus changing simultaneously people's experience of themselves and of what is possible socially. Dialogue is likened to jazz ensemble improvisation, but with the caveat that this is more difficult in the language of words than in music.

What is different?

I have never worked with David Bohm, but I have had the opportunity to talk at some length with his long-time colleague at Birkbeck, Basil Hiley (Bohm and Hiley, 1993) who collaborated with Bohm in his scientific work. I was struck by Hiley's description of the way Bohm clearly struggled to translate the difficult material coming out of quantum physics into insights that would shift our perceptions of 'reality'.

Unlike many other scientists, he was not satisfied with the proposal that only the language of mathematics could express these findings and he was acutely aware of the conflicts between different scientists' views of what quantum theory might mean. He spent a lot of time pondering the paradoxes of the experiments with the nature of light, that sometimes seemed to have a wave-like nature and sometimes a particulate nature depending on the way the experiments were set up and conducted. It was this struggle that led him to propose his theory of the implicate order, a patterned invisible wholeness out of which manifestations unfold into the visible and are then enfolded back again. Reality then consists of an explicate order in which things may appear to be fragmented and unconnected, unfolding out of a deeper implicate order which is a flowing process of unbroken wholeness. Although he was a radical thinker, Bohm did seem to sustain one tradition of scientific thought in which the appearance of paradox indicated a problem in thinking itself. His proposal of the implicate order was a proposal for resolving the paradox of light having a dual nature.

Bohm found resonances in the ideas of his friend, the psychiatrist Patrick de Mare (1991) who was working with the free flow of conversation in groups, what he called 'socio-therapy', as a break-away movement from the tradition of one-to-one psychoanalytic therapy based on Freud's work. This was linked to the school of Group Analysis, particularly associated with Foulkes (1948) where the concept of the group matrix became a key idea, by which participants were conceived as nodes in a field of communication. De Mare also introduced Bohm to the idea of a dialogue group as a 'microculture'. This makes an analogy to a hologram, where the sampling of an entire culture, national or organizational, for example, might be thought to exist in a group of twenty or so people, thereby charging it with multiple views and value systems. He proposed that repeated experience of participating in such sessions led to the emergence of what he called 'impersonal fellowship', an atmosphere of openness and trust that did not depend on members sharing extensive personal history. Bohm's vision of dialogue involved free-flowing communication amongst a group meeting regularly in a circle with no agenda, no purpose, no hierarchy, no authority, 'an empty place'. In this process, he theorized, people come to share a tacit pool of common meaning and coherence (akin to his idea of the implicate order), as they attend to the flow of *apparent* fragmentation of their assumptions, as these emerge from this unbroken wholeness into thought, language and overt expression (akin to the explicate order).

Again what I am pointing to is the particular way of accounting for what may be happening in free-flowing conversation that is being proposed here, which again makes central the idea of a whole beneath, behind or beyond direct interaction as essential to an understanding of the patterning of that interaction. Participation for Bohm means partaking of common meaning or a common mind that arises *between* the individual and the collective, creating a whole that is constantly moving towards coherence. This way of making sense then infuses the work that Isaacs explores in his organizational consulting and facilitating. This leads him to pay a lot of attention to developing people's capacity to engage in dialogue as a special practice or discipline, involving learning through repeated experience the capacity to 'listen', 'suspend', 'respect' and 'voice', where each of these arts has a very particular meaning and theoretical foundation. In fact he sees this in a very similar way to Scharmer. Isaacs also emphasizes the need for a group to return regularly to the dialogue mode as they slowly develop the dialogue 'container'. The disciplines of dialogue allow people to share and tap a tacit pool of coherent meaning, in which the tensions of difference are resolved because they are held together as aspects of a larger unity. This emphasis on differences contained within a larger whole also means that Isaacs favours the introduction of various models such as David Kantor's 'four player system'. This offers a map of the structured repetitive patterns of conversation, the different kinds of roles that such structures require and the way people with certain preferences of style may take up those roles. The same kind of proposal is made for different qualities or 'fields of conversation', different kinds of language. All these *generalized* differences which people easily recognize are all seen to integrate potentially into a coherent whole.

Since I am making sense differently of the way continuity and change emerge spontaneously in human communication, I am not trying to foster a special form or discipline of conversation. I do encourage people to rely less on pre-set agendas and ready made presentations and to engage one another in exploratory conversation that generates stability and potential shifts in what we are holding one another to and how we are doing that. Rather than inculcating a special discipline of dialogue, I am encouraging a perception of ensemble improvisation as an organizing craft of communicative action.

Communities of practice

Etienne Wenger proposes two views of an organization. There is the designed organization, which he calls *the institution* to distinguish it from the organization as lived in practice, and there are the *constellations of intersecting practices* which gives life to the organization. Communities of practice, he says, may be in part a response to but never the direct result of the designed organization (1999: 241). These communities of practice emerge from the local social engagement of people in the day-to-day conduct of some kind of joint enterprise. They are self-organizing, arising, evolving and dissolving according to their own learning, negotiating their own enterprise and shaping their own boundaries of membership, even though all this may be in response to institutional prescriptions, planned events and assigned boundaries. Pursuing practices 'always involves the same kind of embodied, delicate, active, negotiated, complex process of participation.' This participation is understood as the process of producing meaning – meaningful identities, meaningful activities, meaningful ways of accounting to one another for what we are doing, the meaning we give to artefacts and resources.

This perspective allows Wenger to offer an image of organization different from that familiar to most organizational members. The institutional aspect is not an umbrella or overarching structure which unifies the constellations of communities of practice clustering beneath it. Organizational design is rather understood by Wenger as a method by which a set of practices manages itself as a constellation. The designed institution 'does not sit on top; it moves in between. It does not unify by transcending; it connects and disconnects. It does not reign; it travels, to be shaped and appropriated in the context of specific practices' (ibid.: 247). Wenger imagines the work of designing an institution as itself the enterprise of a particular community of practice within a set of practices. This may well be, but is not necessarily or exclusively, that of 'management'. He points out that the work of this community of practice is as local as that of any other. The institutional design is not to be mistaken for a global overview of the constellation of practices, no one can have such a global perspective because the scope of mutual social engagement is always limited. The global is always emergent and beyond design. Thus practice, itself a global phenomena, is not amenable to design. 'One can articulate patterns or define procedures, but neither pattern nor procedures produce the practice as it unfolds. One can design systems of accountability and policies for communities of practice to live by, but one cannot design the practices that will emerge in response to such institutional systems. One can design roles, but not the identities that will be constructed through those roles. One can produce affordances for the negotiation of meaning, but not meaning itself . . .' (ibid.: 229). What we *may* be able to do, Wenger suggests, is learn to design in the service of practice, to support the knowledgeability of practice that is continuously created and reproduced in the process of social engagement. Wenger makes his contribution by articulating a move away from managing organizations as a 'plan of action' and instead as a 'constellation of practices'. His work greatly enriches the concept of the learning organization by discussing a conceptual architecture which may resource conversations about the ongoing definition of an enterprise by those engaged in pursuing it. He disentangles notions of design from any kind of blueprint for organizational practice and so fosters intelligent reflection on the inherently uncertain relationship between our grasp of organizations as designed institutions and our experience of the patterning of organizational activity.

What sounds similar?

Wenger's ideas about the nature of organizations as constellations of communities of practice generated in the process of human sense-making, have much resonance with the perspective of this book series. This resonance comes from a similar understanding of learning and identity formation as a social process. The similarity of our ways of thinking here is clear in relation to Lave and Wenger's earlier writing on situated learning (1991). They develop a theory of *legitimate peripheral participation*, the process by which 'the production, transformation and change in the identities of persons, knowledgeability in practice and communities of practice are realised in the lived-in world of engagement in everyday activity' (ibid.: 47). Their focus of interest bears many similarities to the theorizing in terms of *complex responsive processes of relating* which this book series develops.

Lave and Wenger focus on learning and knowing as social participation, in which person, activity and world are mutually constitutive, rather than on cognitive processes or conceptual structures. We do not learn *about* a practice, they say. Our learning, as the experience of engaging day-to-day as bodily persons in sustaining and developing meaningful activity with others, *is* practice. Practice and personal identity emerge together as our experience of co-created patterns of meaning. Lave and Wenger question the validity of descriptions of social behaviour based on the enactment of prefabricated codes, rules or structures. They reject classical structural analysis where behaviour is explained and serves as empirical evidence for pre-existing, 'underlying' systems. They move away from seeing learning as located in an individual mind that acquires mastery over processes of reasoning and description by internalizing and manipulating structures. As Hanks remarks in his foreword to *Situated Learning*, we do not learn a repertoire of participation schemata; rather, we learn to *do* practices as modes of co-participation. This involves, he suggests, the ability to improvise together. We do not require a commonality of symbolic or referential structures to co-participate. Language here is not a code for *talking about* but is a means of *acting* in the world. Participation is always based on situated negotiation and renegotiation of meaning in the world. 'The notion of participation thus dissolves dichotomies between cerebral and embodied activity, between contemplation and involvement, between abstraction and experience; persons, actions and the world are implicated in all thought, speech, knowing and learning' (Lave and Wenger, 1991: 52).

In my view Lave and Wenger come close to positing the same kind of transformative teleology which we introduced in Volume 1 of this series. Their interest is in how to theorize about the conflictual nature of ordinary, everyday social practice in a way that claims a common process inherent in the simultaneous production of changing persons and changing practice over time. Thus, the transformation of the social order is linked to the immediacy of persons relating as part of situated activity through understanding learning as a process that incorporates meaning-making, politics and the formation of social identity. Because Wenger is explicitly moving away from thinking in terms of systems, he does not make the move I discussed above to creating an *as if* unity of purposefulness of formative teleology for thinking about communities of practice. He is thus in no danger of romanticizing notions of community.

However, as Hanks points out, the theory of legitimate peripheral participation posits a learning process through which the continuity and transformation of the identities of persons, the skills they are mastering and the larger community of practice is necessarily *entailed* by the relational, historical, decentring theorizing, but not *explained*. Theorizing in terms of complex responsive processes of relating does attempt such an explanation. It does this by incorporating the analogy from edge of chaos complex digital simulations of the inherent capacity of iterative, non-linear interaction to pattern itself. It then translates that analogy to the domain of human communication by drawing on Elias's (1970) ideas of power figurations and Mead's (1970) ideas of the evolution of mind, self and society in the complex human conversation of gestures.

What's different?

As Wenger takes up and develops the ideas of communities of practice in relation to institutional design, he seems to move away from the potential paradoxes of transformative teleology implicit in a liberal reading of the earlier writing. In order to discuss ways of designing institutions in terms of conceptual learning architectures or infrastructures, he starts to introduce the logic of dualities. Organisations, he suggests, are best understood as the interaction of two aspects which influence one another, but which maintain their own integrity as sources of structure, one designed and the other emergent. Institution and practice cannot merge because they are different entities that complement one another: 'The point of design is to make organisations ready for the emergent by serving the inventiveness of practice and the potential for innovation inherent in its emergent structure' (ibid.: 245).

Although Wenger states that institutional design is a practice of a community of practice like any other, his interest is exploring the rationality of design as a set of macro concepts, not the political learning processes in which any particular design emerges. In doing this he loses the paradoxical relationship between design and emergence which I have wished to preserve because my focus of interest is on how particular forms of institutionalization are emerging in the social engagement in which I have been invited to participate. Wenger approaches this when he says that the designed institution and the emergent constellation of communities of practice exist in a tension that cannot be resolved once and for all. Rather, he understands the evolution of an organization as the constant renegotiation of the alignment between institution and constellations of lived practices through the negotiation of meaning.

Once again in pursuit of his interests in macro concepts of design, he introduces another duality to explain what he means by the negotiation of meaning: that of participation and reification. What Wenger seems to be saying is this. In their participation as members of a community of practice, in their acting and their interacting, people are producing

reifications on which they focus attention and enable sharing in their participation. By reification Wenger includes far more than artefacts. So, for example, when people are interrelating with each other through talking, say, they are projecting meanings onto 'objects' that their interaction is producing, say plans, stories, gestures, silences, glances. These reifications then offer a focus of attention around which further negotiation of these projected meanings can be organized. Taken together as a unity, this dual process of participation (mutual recognition of each other) and reification (projecting meaning onto 'objects') constitutes the negotiation of meaning, which is essentially what a practice is, producing both novelty and continuity. Thus Wenger explains the emergence of meaning as a participative process that both produces and uses reification. There is a sense of participation and reification taking place at the same time but as the interplay of distinct but complementary processes, occurring in different realms, which together constitute an inseparable interwoven unity. This differs from the explanation of the emergence of meaning as the movement of a paradoxical dialectic as in Mead's theory of the emergence of mind, self, and society in the conversation of responsive gesturing. Here meaning emerges *as significant symbols* in the conversation of gestures between interacting bodies. The act of gesturing (moving, talking, doing) is continuously finding its meaning in the response to it, in the context of a history of such responsive gesturing. The paradox of continuity and novelty in the evolution of meaning is created by the way response is always acting back to further shape gesture in the very process of gesturing as well as when a gesture is later appealed to as part of subsequent gesturing.

By explaining the process of meaning as the interplay of a duality, of two distinct but complementary aspects occurring in different realms, Wenger serves his concern to conceptualize institutional design as learning architectures. His explanation of sources of structure in organizations as the interplay of design and emergence, and the other dualities he introduces, serves him in the same way. He can now suggest we ask such questions in relation to institutionalization as:

- what should be institutionalized and when should participation be relied on?
- what forms of participation are required to give meaning to institutional reification?
- how can design be kept to a minimum and still ensure continuity and coherence?
- what are the obstacles to responsiveness to the emergent?

- what are the mechanisms by which emergent patterns can be perceived?
- does the institutional design serve as a communication tool?

The discussion can now reside entirely in rational reflection on what kind of 'lever' we may use to influence the future shape of practice, to maintain the status quo or to redirect the practice. Wenger says: 'You can seek, cultivate, or avoid specific relationships with specific people.' Also, 'You can produce or promote specific artefacts to focus future negotiation of meaning in specific ways' (1999: 91). He also says: 'Because of the complementarity of participation and reification, the two forms of politics can be played off against each other.' 'As a result of this complementarity, control over practice usually requires a grip on both forms of politics . . .' (ibid.: 92).

> Because the negotiation of meaning is the convergence of participation and reification, controlling both participation and reification affords control over the kinds of meaning that can be created in certain contexts and the kind of persons that participants can become . . . The combination of the two forms of politics is powerful indeed when it affords a hold on the development of a practice . . . No form of control over the future can be complete and secured. In order to sustain social coherence of participation and reification within which it can be exercised, control must constantly be reproduced, reasserted, renegotiated in practice.
>
> (ibid.: 93)

When Wenger does offer us insight into the interactive detail by which communities of practice are emerging as political sense-making processes, he takes the classic ethnographic position. He offers us a composite picture of a 'day in the life' of a claims processor in a large health insurance company, composed from his fieldwork notes. His own engagement in the meaning-making processes of that work at the time are almost entirely missing from his account. He takes us in the direction of investing more attention and care in design rather than in the quality of our ongoing participation in the actual political learning processes themselves. He and I therefore share very similar interests, yet we would draw attention and invite investment differently.

Coda: how do organizations change?

The question, 'How do we go about changing complex organizations?'
often means 'How can we formulate intentions and communicate them as
agreed plans of action to be implemented?' In other words, it involves
conceiving a future different in some way from a conception of the past
and taking action to realize the change. The focus is then often on
providing tools to help produce conceptions of both the content and the
process of change – survey instruments, diagnostic and strategic
frameworks, system models, visioning aids, simulations, planning tools,
interactive technologies, process designs and change methodologies.
Such books on organizational change help us with tools for giving birth
to our ideas about what and how to change. They help us to step back and
frame a view of ourselves in our situation with all the material,
technological, cultural and political factors that we may need to take into
account. They are tools to help us as participant-observers in
organizational change. The more sophisticated tools help us frame views
of ourselves in the very act of doing the framing, so that they become
reflexive tools to help us as participant-conceptualizers.

In this book I have been asking and exploring a rather different question.
I have been asking, 'How do we participate in the way things change
over time?' meaning 'How at the very movement of our joint sense-
making experience, are we changing ourselves and our situation?'
This means inquiring into the ongoing local situated communicative
activity between experiencing bodies that gives rise to intentions,
decisions and actions, tool-making and tool-using. Such an approach
attempts to explore the paradox that our interaction, no matter how
considered or passionate, is always evolving in ways that we cannot
control or predict in the longer term, no matter how sophisticated our
planning tools.

I have suggested working iteratively with such questions as:

'Who are we realizing we are as we gather here?'
'What kind of sense are we making together?'
'What are we coming to talk about as we converse?'
'How are we shifting our understanding of what we are engaged in?'
'What kind of enterprise are we shaping?'

The movement of sense-making I keep illustrating is not a steady move towards a unified 'we' constructing consensus and common ground as a basis for joint action. Rather I have referred to the inevitable conflictual nature of organizing our immediate next step as difference, misunderstanding and plurality emerge in webs of interconnected relating. Emerging coherence here does mean integration into a unified whole, but is inherent in the self-organizing nature of interaction amongst differences. Since it is the webs of enabling constraints of a material, political and cultural nature that we are continuously recreating and potentially shifting, our interaction is at work creating continuity and change at all scales simultaneously. This happens as the patterning of interaction is amplified and damped over time as interaction continues.

I have sought to shift the current emphasis of strategic work in organizations described in terms of conceptual ability brought to bear on the large-scale combined with individual skills of communication exercised at the small-scale. I am saying that this is not an adequate description or account of how organizations and other social forms evolve, disappear and appear. I am encouraging us to experience the paradox of forming and being formed as situated social selves, emerging persons in emerging social worlds patterned by history but open to movement as present interaction. Thus I am drawing attention to organizations and ourselves in the process of changing as we live our lives together. Although I emphasize the constantly recurring potential for change as we interact, what I am drawing attention to is as much an account of the potential for repetition and recurrence. Our human capacity for narrative sense-making means we create our sense of continuity and change, stability and instability as a single movement of living experience.

I have wanted to give much more emphasis to strategic work as the living craft of participating as an intentional fellow sense-maker in conversation after conversation (both public and imagined), encounter after encounter, activity after activity. I want to help us appreciate ourselves as fellow improvisers in ensemble work, constantly constructing the future and our part in it as daily activity as we convene or join or unexpectedly find ourselves in conversations. I have called this a craft because, just as we can learn to conceptualize, to design, to communicate and persuade, we can also learn to participate with imaginative concreteness as co-narrators, joint authors, co-improvisers, and in so doing, locate our competence as leaders differently. Although I have described my own work in terms of a different account of process consultation, what I am saying is as relevant to anyone wanting to think about their participation in organizational life.

Appendix: a cast list for Ferrovia (in order of appearance)

Alessandro	Manager in Technical Support to the Film Business at the plant.
Stefano	Head of Management Development at the plant.
Franco	Youngest manager on the Site Management Committee.
Cesare	Recently appointed to head Quality Improvement Project.
Donald	Managing Director for Europe.
Carlo	Head of Manufacturing at the plant.
Louisa	Young research scientist.
Piero	Junior Manager in the Research Labs.
Lorenzo	Another young research scientist.
Eduardo	Senior Manager of Research Labs and member of Site Committee.
Roberto	Senior Manager of Research Labs and member of Site Committee.
Fulvio	Member of Site Committee.
Maurizio	Manager of Italian Operation of parent company.
Giorgio	Head of the plant's Site Management Committee.
Alberto	Head of Management Development for Italian operation.
Gianni	Research scientist in chemical processing.
Walter	Young manager in the film business.
Simona	Young manager in the film business.
Bob	Seconded from US to implement new IT systems.

References

Argyris, C. (1982) *Reasoning, Learning and Action*. San Francisco, CA: Jossey Bass.

Argyris, C., Putman, R. and Smith, D.M. (1985) *Action Science: Concepts, Methods and Skills for Research and Intervention*. San Francisco, CA: Jossey-Bass.

Bateson, G. (1973) *Steps to an Ecology of Mind*. St Albans: Paladin.

Beckhard, R. (1969) *Organization Development: Strategies and Models*. Reading, MA: Addison-Wesley.

Bennett, S. and Brown, J. (1998) 'Mindshift: Strategic Dialogue for Breakthrough Thinking', in *Learning Organisations*.

Bennis, W.G. (1969) *Organization Development: its Nature, Origins, and Prospects*. Reading, MA: Addison-Wesley.

Bion, W. (1961) *Experiences in Groups and Other Papers*. London: Tavistock Publications.

Blake, R.R. and Mouton, J. (1969) *Building a Dynamic Corporation through Grid Organization Development*. Reading, MA: Addison-Wesley.

Boal, A. (1998) *Legislative Theatre*. London: Routledge.

Bohm, D. (1980) *Wholeness and the Implicate Order*. London: Routledge.

Bohm, D. (1987) *Unfolding Meaning*. London: Routledge.

Bohm, D. (1994) *Thought as a System*. London: Routledge.

Bohm, D. (1999) *On Dialogue*. London: Routledge.

Bohm, D. and Hiley, B.J. (1993) *The Undivided Universe: an Ontological Interpretation of Quantum Theory*. London: Routledge.

Brook, P. (1990) *The Empty Space*. London: Penguin.

Capra, F. (1996) *The Web of Life*. London: HarperCollins.

Checkland, P. (1981) *Systems Thinking, Systems Practice*. New York, NY: John Wiley. JAI Press.

Churchman, C.W. (1968) *The Systems Approach*. New York, NY: Delacourt Press.

Clarkson, P. and Shaw, P. (1992) 'Human Relationships at Work – The Place of Counselling Skills and Consulting Skills and Services in Organizations', *MEAD: The Journal of the Association of Management Education and Development* 23, 10: 18–29.

Elias, N. (1970) *What is Sociology?* New York, NY: Columbia University Press.

Foulkes, S.H. (1948) *Introduction to Group Analytic Therapy*. London: Heinemann Medical Books.

Goodwin, B. (1994) *How the Leopard Changed its Spots: The Evolution of Complexity*. London: Weidenfeld & Nicolson.

Griffin, D. (2001) *The Emergence of Leadership: Linking Self-organization and Ethics*. London: Routledge.

Hamel, G. and Prahalad, C.K. (1994) *Competing for the Future*. Boston, MA: Harvard Business School Press.

Hampden-Turner, C. (1994) *Corporate Culture*. London: Priatkus.

Ison, R. and Russell, D. (2000) *Agricultural Extension and Rural Development: Breaking out of Traditions*. Cambridge: Cambridge University Press.

Isaacs, W. (1999) *Dialogue and the Art of Thinking Together*. New York, NY: Currency/Doubleday.

James, W. (1890) *Principles of Psychology, vols 1 and 2*. London: Macmillan.

Johnstone, K. (1989) *Impro: Improvisation and the Theatre*. London: Methuen.

Kauffman, S. (1995) *At Home in the Universe: The Search for the Laws of Complexity*. London: Viking.

Kofman, F. and Senge, P.M. (1993) 'Communities of Commitment: the Heart of Learning Organizations', in *Journal of American Management Association* 12–30.

Kolb, D.A. (1984) *Experiential Learning: Experience as the Source of Learning and Development*. New York: Prentice-Hall.

Lane, D. and Maxfield, R. (1996) 'Strategy Under Complexity', *Foresight, Complexity and Strategy in Long Range Planning* 29, 2.

Langton, G.C. (1992) 'Life at the Edge of Chaos', in Langton, G.C., Doyne Farmer, J. and Rasmussen, S. (eds) *Artificial Life II, Santa Fe Institute, Studies in the Sciences of Complexity, vol. 10*. Reading, MA: Addison-Wesley.

Lave, J. and Wenger, E. (1991) *Situated Learning: Legitimate Peripheral Participation*. Cambridge: Cambridge University Press.

Lawrence, P.R. and Lorsch, J.W. (1969) *Developing Organizations: Diagnosis and Action*. Reading, MA: Addison-Wesley.

Lewin, K. (1946) 'Action Research and Minority Problems', *Journal of Social Issues* 2: 34–36.

Lewin, R. and Regine, B. (2000) *The Soul at Work*. London: Orion Business Books.

Lovelock, J. (1979) *A New Look at Life on Earth*. Oxford: Oxford University Press.

Lovelock, J. (1991) *Gaia: The Practical Science of Planetary Medicine*. London: Gaia Books.

de Mare, P., Piper, R. and Thompson, S. (1991) *Koinonia*. London: Karnac.

Maturana, H. and Varela, F.J. (1992) *The Tree of Knowledge: the Biological Roots of Human Understanding*. Boston, MA: Shambala.

Mead, G.H. (1970) *Mind, Self and Society*. Chicago, IL: University of Chicago Press.

Morgan, G. (1986) *Images of Organization*. Beverly Hills, CA: Sage.

Nevis, E.C. (1987) *Organizational Consulting: a Gestalt Approach*. New York, NY: Gardner Press.

Owen, H. (1992, 2nd edition 1997) *Open Space Technology: a User's Guide*. San Francisco, CA: Berrett-Koehler.

Polster, E. and Polster, M. (1973) *Gestalt Therapy Integrated*. New York, NY: Brunner/Mazel.

Prigogine, I. and Stengers, I. (1984) *Order Out of Chaos*. New York, NY: Bantam Books.

Prigogine, I. (1997) *The End of Certainty: Time, Chaos and the New Laws of Nature*. New York, NY: The Free Press.

Ray, T.S. (1992) 'An Approach to the Synthesis of Life', in Langton, G.C., Taylor, C., Dyne-Farmer, J. and Rasmussen, S. (eds) *Artificial Life II, Santa Fe Institute, Studies in the Sciences of Complexity, vol. 10*. Reading, MA: Addison-Wesley.

Scharmer, C.O. (2000*) Presencing: Using the Self as Gate for the Coming-Into-Presence of the Future*. Paper for conference on Knowledge and Innovation, May 25–6, 2000, Helsinki, Finland.

Schein, E.H. (1987) *Process Consultation, vol. 2: Lessons for Managers and Consultants*. Reading, MA: Addison-Wesley.

Schein, E.H. (1988, 2nd edition) *Process Consultation: its Role in Organization Development*. Reading, MA: Addison-Wesley.

Schon, D.A. (1987) *Educating the Reflective Practitioner: Towards a New Design for Teaching and Learning in the Professions*. San Fransisco, CA: Jossey Bass.

Senge, P.M. (1990) *The Fifth Discipline: The Art and Practice of the Learning Organisation*. New York, NY: Doubleday.

Senge, P., Kleiner, K., Roberts, C., Ross, R., Roth, G. and Smith, B. (1999) *The Dance of Change*. London: Nicholas Brealey.

Shaw, P. (1997) 'Intervening in the Shadow Systems of Organizations: Consulting from a Complexity Perspective', *Journal of Organizational Change Management* 10, 3: 235–250.

Shotter, J. (1984) *Social Accountability and Selfhood*. Oxford: Blackwell.

Shotter, J. (1993) *Conversational Realities: Constructing Life through Language*. London: Sage.

Stacey, R.D., Griffin, D. and Shaw, P. (2000) *Complexity and Management: Fad or Radical Challenge to Systems Thinking?* London: Routledge.

Stacey, R.D. (2001) *Complex Responsive Processes in Organizations: Learning and Knowledge Creation*. London: Routledge.

Tatham, P. (1998) 'The Social Dreaming Matrix', in Lawrence, W.G. (ed.) *Social Dreaming @ Work*. London: Karnac Books.

Trist, F.E. and Emery, E.L. (1973) *Toward a Social Psychology*. New York, NY: Plenum.

Trompenaars, F. (1993) *Riding the Waves of Culture*. London: Economist Books.

Varela, F., Maturana, H. and Uribe, R. (1974) 'Autopoiesis: The Organization of Living Systems, its Characterisation and a Model', in *Biosystems*, vol. 5, 187–196.

Von Bertalanffy, L. (1952) *General Systems Theory*. New York, NY: Wiley.

Waldrop, M.M. (1992) *Complexity: the Emerging Science at the Edge of Chaos*. New York, NY: Simon and Schuster.

Walton, R.E. (1969) *Interpersonal Peacemaking: Confrontations and Third-Party Consultation*. Reading, MA: Addison-Wesley.

Weick, K.E. (1995) *Sensemaking in Organizations*. Thousand Oaks, CA: Sage.

Weisbord, M.R. (ed.) (1992) *Discovering Common Ground*. San Francisco, CA: Berrett-Koehler.

Weisbord, M.R. and Janoff, S. (1995, 2nd edition 2000) *Future Search: an Action Guide to Finding Common Ground in Organizations and Communities*. San Francisco, CA: Berrett-Koehler.

Wenger, E. (1999) *Communities of Practice: Learning, Meaning and Identity*. Cambridge: Cambridge University Press.

Wheatley, M.J. (1992) *Leadership and the New Science: Learning About Organization from an Orderly Universe*. San Francisco, CA: Berrett-Koehler.

Wheatley, M.J. and Kellner-Rogers, M. (1996) *A Simpler Way*. San Francisco, CA: Berrett-Koehler.

Index